One Year After

From Grief to Hope

ELLY SHEYKHET

ONE YEAR AFTER: FROM GRIEF TO HOPE

Published by
Alina's Light Publishing

Printed in the United States of America

ISBN: 978-1-62375-163-0

Cover design by Publish Assist
Edited by Cori Wamsley

www.alinaslight.com

DEDICATION

This book is dedicated to my daughter and all the beautiful children who have left this world at a young age. My daughter is one of many spirit warriors that so many of us need to believe in. She has taught me how to love deeply and be more compassionate, how to appreciate and be grateful for what you have, and how to forgive and not judge. The spirit of my beautiful daughter is a shining light in the middle of darkness. Her light makes me shine in a way I never knew possible.

Alina Sheykhet, a shining light, 1997–2017

Table of Contents

Introduction

I am a mother whose daughter was brutally murdered. I am not a professional writer, and English is my second language. Even in my own language, I have never possessed exceptional writing skills. I am just one bereaved mother with a broken heart, living my life that's been forever changed and trying to help those who were thrown onto a path of life that feels impossible to survive. I wrote this book to deliver a message of hope to other grieving parents. It is my wish that my story will become part of someone else's survival guide and give people a better understanding of how they can help their families and friends who are suffering the loss of their loved ones.

*   *   *

My husband Yan, our kids Artem and Alina, and I came to the United States from Russia in December of 2000. Our son was 8 years old, and Alina was only 3. America welcomed us, and we believed that living here would open doors and create opportunities and possibilities for us to build a happy life with a promising future for our kids. The language barrier made it more difficult to travel through those doors, and we all had to work and study hard.

Over the years, my husband and I built a solid foundation for our kids to start independent lives of their own. By 2017, our kids had accomplished so much. Our son graduated from college, got a good job, got married, and was enjoying a happy life with his wife, Kate, and their newborn daughter, Angelina. Our daughter, a talented performer on many stages, was a junior at the University of Pittsburgh, studying to become a doctor of physical therapy. Vibrant, sensitive, and beautiful, she was suddenly taken away from us at the age of 20. And with that, our happy lives and promising futures ended.

I have been asked many times how I was able to continue my life after it turned in such an unimaginable direction. In this book, I want to reveal how I survived after discovering the breathless body of my child. I want to share all the feelings, emotions, and experiences that I faced in the year following her death.

My story is very raw. Part I describes the events that took place three days before Yan and I found Alina in her apartment. Based on my text message exchanges with Alina, I was able to build a chronology of how she spent the last three days of her life. My story reveals her last words to us and what she was doing in her last hours. Also, Part I reveals many details of the day of the tragedy and a few days after until the day of Alina's funeral.

In Part II, I unveil my roadmap for navigating this new world without my child. I have faced and overcome so many challenges after burying my daughter, and these challenges have allowed me to open my mind and soul to new experiences. I have developed a different understanding of life and death and have come to find myself fluttering between two worlds—a physical world and a spiritual world.

*   *   *

The most painful thing that can happen to any parent is the loss of a child. That loss turns people's lives to ruins. Even if you stay rooted in the physical world, your life is divided into two parts: the "Before" and the "After." You become a different person, and you can pinpoint the exact moment you lost the old "you."

But even with all the pain and grief, I am living proof that survival is possible. When you are confronted with the intense suffering that comes with losing a child, you can live in the memories of the love that you shared. The greatest power that we possess is the power of love. It gives us strength and forces us to continue living even when we feel like dying.

PART I: BEFORE

Chapter 1: The Unthinkable

Thursday, October 5th

Yan and I parked at Alina's house in Oakland, and I texted her to come out. We waited for a few minutes before the door opened and our daughter appeared. She looked beautiful and mature, but her body language expressed the anxiety running through her head. I felt it too, and the sight of her filled me with mixed emotions. Despite her nerves, a strong young lady walked to our car.

Alina got in the car and simply said, "Hi, guys." It was unusual for her to be this short; we would typically laugh and goof around together. I knew she was nervous but was trying not to make it obvious. I jokingly said, "Wow, Alina, are you my daughter?"

She smirked. "Mom! Stop!" With that, we left Alina's apartment and began our mostly silent car ride to the courthouse.

We entered the building, our second time there ever. As we stood in line to go through security, we looked at each other and tried not to laugh. We started whispering about the last time we were in that building, when Alina tried to go through the security line with pepper spray in her purse. We giggled, remembering how mad the security lady was when she found the spray, which was strictly prohibited in that building, and how they had to check Alina's criminal record prior to allowing her inside.

Mortified and annoyed, Alina said, "Oh my God, Mom, I can't believe I forgot about that stupid spray and how dumb that made me look." Then she gave me a funny look and said, "And you, Mom, happened to have a freaking pizza in your purse, which was embarrassing too." Yan was behind us, watching our conversation and rolling his eyes, shaking his head and smiling, no doubt thinking how much he adored his two silly girls.

We entered an elevator, and a gentleman in a business suit asked if we needed directions. Alina immediately took responsibility. She said that she had a hearing scheduled and asked what floor we should proceed to. The gentleman looked at her with a very kind smile and explained where to go. I was amazed by how my daughter had presented herself. She was my child, my baby girl, and I was mesmerized by her mature look. I had a feeling that her manners, her voice, and her confidence made the gentleman think that she was an attorney.

She checked in, and we were directed to a waiting room. The moment we entered that room, I felt very uncomfortable. I looked around, acknowledging just one thought running through my head: "What are we doing here? Why are we even here?" Every single cell in my body felt that we didn't belong there.

*   *   *

Two weeks earlier, Alina had woken up in the night to find her ex-boyfriend, Matthew Darby, in her bedroom. He had climbed up the gutter and entered the home through the second-floor kitchen window. Alina had dated Darby previously but broke up with him when he became controlling and manipulative. He refused to accept her decision to break up and would not stop contacting her, so she blocked his number. As he stood in her bedroom that night after breaking into her house, he demanded that she talk to him. She cried out for her roommates, and they called the police. But Darby fled the scene.

Alina filed a petition for an Order for Protection from Abuse ("PFA"), which would prohibit Darby from speaking to her or going near her. At the hearing for the temporary PFA, Alina told the judge that she did not believe that Darby wanted to harm her but that he was controlling. She was also concerned because there was an active arrest warrant for Darby. The judge expressed a serious concern for her safety and granted the temporary PFA. Her final PFA hearing was scheduled for October 5th.

When I talked to her after the temporary PFA was granted, I asked her how she could be sure that he would not try to meet her somewhere and hurt her. She gave me a "you-don't-know-what-you're-talking-about" look. With such confidence in her voice, she replied, "No, Mom, he just can't. He is not allowed to." She felt very safe, and she trusted the law to protect her. Yan and I were not educated on relationship abuse or PFAs at all, and we simply trusted our daughter. We truly believed that the PFA would stop Darby from bothering her and that he would leave her alone.

*   *   *

As we sat in the waiting room, we observed our surroundings. There were so many people, and every single face expressed sadness, worry, fear, and concern. Alina was quietly inspecting the crowd, looking for Darby. We did not know at the time that victims and defendants had separate waiting rooms. I could feel that she was nervous and uncomfortable, too.

Alina's name was called, and we proceeded to an office. A young lady walked in shortly after and introduced herself as Sasha Phillips, the attorney assigned to Alina's case. Alina explained what had happened to her and what she had done to file for a PFA. Once again, I was amazed by how beautiful, mature, and eloquent my child was.

Sasha made a few calls and informed us that Darby was never served with the petition so the hearing could not go forward. We were so confused about how this could happen. Alina had filed her PFA petition on September 21st, and it was now October 5th. How could he not have been served during that two-week period?

Sasha advised Alina to file all the paperwork again and suggested that we go to a police station and hand the forms to them. Sasha asked us to sit in the waiting room so she could reschedule the hearing. Overwhelmed with disappointment and disbelief, we sat in the waiting room again. We both were silent. I could feel how sad Alina was. She held my hand and cried. "Mom, I am so tired. I don't want any of this. I just want him to leave me alone. I have asked him nicely so many times, but he refuses to understand. I still care for him, Mom, and I wish him the best in life. I just want him to leave me alone. He needs to understand that, Mom."

My heart was breaking for her. I could feel her pain but could not find the right words to respond to her tears and just kept saying that it all would be over soon and that she would forget about everything and be happy again. A few minutes later, Sasha returned and told us that the hearing was rescheduled for October 10th. She wished Alina good luck and said that she would see her in a few days.

Alina never had the chance to see Sasha again and learn that she was, in fact, Russian, as I thought when I first heard her name. Alina was very proud of her heritage and loved being a Russian girl. She would have been touched that someone who shared her heritage wanted to help her.

Interestingly, I later learned that Sasha had been touched by Alina's story. A few months after Alina's death, Sasha painted a beautiful portrait of Alina, arms outstretched with flames rising from her hands. She said Alina's spirit helped her create this powerful artwork.

We exited the courthouse and immediately felt relieved when we took a deep breath of fresh fall air. As we walked away from that unpleasant place, a feeling of normalcy slowly filled me again. We looked at each other and smiled, silently agreeing that it felt nice leaving that gloomy building behind. Yan was waiting outside, and when we got in his car, Alina started venting. "Dad, you would not believe what just happened. We have to go to the police station now!" She got very emotional and kept asking why Darby had not been served and how he could have gotten out of jail so easily.

This was when she revealed to us that Darby had some other pending criminal charges. She told us that, at the time that Darby broke into her house, he was already on probation. She knew that he had been arrested and charged with criminal trespass and thought that another bond could not be granted. She had been surprised to learn that his father was able to bail him out of jail again. "He's already out on bail for something else. Sorry I didn't tell you, but instead of serving him with the PFA or keeping him in jail forever, they let him out. Why in the world would they bail him out?" She raged about how the system was messed up and vowed that if she ever had the chance, she would change it.

*   *   *

We entered the building where the Zone 4 Police Department was located, and our frustrations continued. We were greeted by two police officers, and Alina explained what kind of help she sought. After she finished her story, one officer looked at her papers and laughed. "Of course we were not able to serve Darby. You did not write down his address!"

Alina's eyes widened. "I don't know his home address, but I indicated his location and that he is a student of UPG." He went to the University of Pittsburgh's Greensburg campus.

The officer sneered. "He is not even located in Pittsburgh? Go to a police station in Greensburg, and hand all these papers to them." Alina had started her college career at the Pitt-Greensburg campus and just recently transferred to the Oakland campus, which is in Pittsburgh.

I was speechless. Alina looked at me and rolled her eyes. We both felt confused and helpless.

Alina took a deep breath. "Excuse me, guys. Don't you think it should be your responsibility to find his address? You are the police, and I am the victim here. I am asking for help." She sounded sweet as usual, but you could not miss the light sarcasm in her voice.

The officer responded, "Sure, we can call the Greensburg police station for you. Do you have a number to dial?" We could not believe what we had just heard. I never expected to be faced with such carelessness and unprofessionalism by the police.

Alina raised her voice. "I am sorry, sir. I don't carry the yellow pages with me, and I would assume that you guys would know how to call each other to help us citizens."

The other officer overheard Alina's statement and offered his help. He looked into Darby's record but didn't find anything. He couldn't explain why Darby's record was clear when he had been arrested and placed in jail just days before. The only explanation he could give was that the other charges may have been filed in a different county, so Allegheny County was not aware of them. The officer advised us that he would call the Greensburg station and fax all the documents over shortly. We thanked him for his help, wished everyone a nice day, and left.

As we left the police station, Alina said, "Wow, I was not even safe this whole time!"

My daughter was overwhelmed with disappointment and frustration. For the whole ride back home, she told her father that she could not believe how unprofessionally she had been treated by the police officer, how the system was messed up, and how she really wanted to change that system so people could feel safe and be more protected.

Friday, October 6th

I did not see Alina until late that evening when Yan and I picked her up from work. Not seeing each other never stopped us from communicating, though. We constantly texted during the day and always stayed connected with the family.

At 9:23 am, we got what we thought was a text with some good news.

Alina: Apparently the hearing has been moved from the 10th to the 17th

Me: Why

Alina: I asked, and he didn't know why

Me: Who's he?

Alina: Officer Grismier called last night

Also he was served with the PFA last night at his work

Me: I see Allegheny police started working

Alina: Finally

It's about freakin time they started doing anything

Yan: Good morning, sounds good

Alina: Good morning

At 11:03 pm, Yan and I waited in front of the Hilton Garden Inn to pick her up from work. She had just gotten a new job at the hotel and absolutely loved it. She worked at the front desk and enjoyed helping the guests. She loved her new co-workers, and in Alina's words, the owner was the "sweetest and cutest old lady she ever met." Alina was very proud to wear a Hilton Garden Inn uniform with a nametag that read, "Ask about my Promise to you. ALINA."

Benji was with us. He is a little Yorkie we had gotten Alina on her 12th birthday. She loved him so much and often referred to him as her son. We knew she would be happy to see him.

Yan and I watched her through the window as she finished up her work at the front desk. We both were mesmerized by her, feeling so much love and admiration for our sweet, beautiful girl. She came out and jumped in the car, happy and bubbly with laughter. She was so excited to see Benji and gave him a million kisses. We parked at her Oakland house. She took the food that we had picked up for her dinner, said "thank you so much," and told us that we were the best parents in the world and she loved us so much. We watched her walk up to the house, assuming she would be safe. She turned around before she went in, waved good night, and disappeared behind the closed door.

Saturday, October 7th

I was babysitting my 3-week-old granddaughter. I was filled with happiness and contentment. Proud to be a grandma at age 45, I smiled, remembering Alina's comment that I was "the hottest grandma ever." In my head, I pictured my future where I had a big family with both my kids happy and satisfied with their lives. I held my precious granddaughter, filled with joy because she looked absolutely beautiful. As I looked at her adorable little face, reflecting on what a blessing she was, I began to wonder what Alina's daughter would look like.

I remembered how Alina was in the delivery room when her niece Angelina entered this world. She had been so excited when Kate, Alina's sister-in-law, chose her as the second person after Artem to be permitted in the room. Alina had been so happy to have this opportunity to support her big brother and his wife at the most important moment of their lives and witness their feelings and emotions. Throughout the delivery, she constantly texted us, informing us of what was happening as we were giddy with anticipation. Yan, Kate's mom, and I had spent two full days in the hospital, never leaving the building. Alina was with us for most of that time. She missed her classes and did her homework at night while the rest of the family tried to get some sleep in the waiting room. The next day, when her professor asked her why she had been absent, she proudly responded, "I was delivering a baby," and the whole class laughed.

I remembered how I almost dropped my phone when the most anticipated text message came through: "She is here; she is beautiful." A few minutes later, Alina came out with the biggest smile on her face, saying, "Oh my God, it was amazing! I had the most precious experience in my life." Then she told us how nice the doctor was and that she had asked the doctor to deliver her baby too. We all laughed.

"Oh my God, I cannot wait to have MY baby," she proudly shrieked. "And you, Mom, will definitely be by my side, holding my hand!" Then she turned to her smiling father and joked, "And you, Dad, will obviously be waiting outside!"

*   *   *

That night, Yan left the house to pick up Alina from work. Because we had to wake up early the next morning to pick Alina and her friends up for the Susan Komen Paws for the Cure Dog Walk, I decided to stay home and get some rest. I regretted that decision later. I wish I had gone with Yan that night and had the chance to see my daughter on her last day with us.

Yan stopped at the pizzeria and got Alina a pepperoni pizza for her dinner. Then he parked in front of the hotel and patiently waited, watching his daughter through the hotel window.

At 11:00 pm, Alina got in the car and said, "Hi, Dad!" She was so happy and bubbly. Everything was going well. She was so excited to eat her pizza and finally get her bank card that Yan had brought her. She had just gotten her first paycheck from the hotel and proudly showed it to her dad while laughing. "Oh my God, Dad, finally I can live again!"

Yan asked her if maybe she wanted to go home with him and spend the night at our house. But she declined, saying that we would have to pick up her friends in the morning anyway, so she would get better sleep at her place.

For the rest of my life I will wish that Yan had brought her home that night.

Yan parked in front of Alina's house. She grabbed her pizza, gave her dad a very tight hug, thanked him, and told him that she loved him and that she would see him in the morning. She jumped out of the car and quickly ran into her house. There was a little framed window at the front door, and when the door closed behind her, Yan looked back to see her happy face pop up in that tiny window. He thought it was very cute and funny; Alina had never done that before. She was playfully smiling at him and gave him a cute wave good night. He waved back to her, whispering that he loved her too and that he would see his silly girl in the morning.

He had no idea that the next morning he would see his silly girl in a way he wasn't expecting, in a way that no parent should ever see their child.

*   *   *

To my own surprise, I was still awake when I heard my phone "ping" at 12:10 am, indicating that I had received a text message. I unlocked my phone, and there was a picture sent from Alina. She was standing in front of the mirror next to the entrance door, the door that had that little framed window through which she had been waving her last goodbye to her daddy an hour ago. She was wearing her hotel uniform, her dark wavy hair falling down her shoulders. She looked beautiful. I could tell she was a little tired but happy. Right behind her was her roommate and best friend, Zach. He was wearing a bright red t-shirt with the Denny's logo on it. He also looked tired but very peaceful.

Me: And where are you two going to?

Or have come from? It's raining!

Alina: We both came home from work around the same time and wanted to take a picture haha

Me: Dusya

Alina had many sweet nicknames. "Dusya" described her as a silly, sweet little girl. She liked when we called her that name. She always giggled at the sound of it, and she knew that such a short and silly sounding word contained so much parental love and expressed how much we adored her.

I turned the light off and started falling asleep. I felt very calm and warm inside. Knowing that both of my kids were happy and content brought me so much peace and joy. I felt like one lucky mother and grandmother and looked forward to having a good time tomorrow.

I had no idea that would be the last time I would feel happy and peaceful. I had no idea that picture would be the last picture my daughter would ever send to me. I had no idea that the next day would change our lives forever.

Sunday, October 8th

7:00 am

The sound of the alarm clock woke me up. I was excited, knowing it was going to be a very good day filled with so much fun and happiness. It was Artem's 25th birthday, and Kate's birthday was just the day before, so we had planned to have a family celebration right after the walk. I didn't want to call my son that early and thought I would put him on speakerphone when Alina got in the car so we could all wish him a happy birthday. I jumped out of bed, screaming, "Yan, get up, we need to get ready!"

7:12 am

I checked my Facebook and noticed a Russian recipe for zucchini pancakes that I thought Alina would like to try. I sent her that recipe through Facebook messenger, and I saw that my message had been read.

8:08 am

Yan and I were about to leave, and I was holding a pink Mickey Mouse hat we had gotten for Alina at Disney World for her 9th birthday. I thought it would be funny if I wore it as my accessory to amplify my very pink outfit. I quickly put the hat on, made a funny face, and took a selfie for Alina.

I sent it to her, expecting to get a "hahaha" reaction. She didn't respond.

8:33 am

Because I still didn't get a response from Alina, which was unusual, I called her to make sure she was awake and getting ready. She did not answer. I assumed she was in the bathroom, so

I called her again after a few minutes, but again, she did not pick up her phone. I hoped she hadn't fallen back asleep, but that would be strange because she was very responsible. I started getting mad, thinking that she and her friends might still be sleeping, and we would be late for the event. I did not think for even a second that my daughter's phone could be miles away from her and that someone else could be reading my messages.

8:45 am

We parked at Alina's house, and I called her again. She did not answer. I got out of the car, complaining to Yan, "Oh my God, they must be out of their minds. We will be so late!"

I knocked on the front door. After a few seconds, Zach opened the door, greeting me with "good morning." He was supposed to go on the walk with us and obviously was not yet ready. The house seemed very quiet. I frantically asked, "Where is Alina? Is Becca awake yet?" Becca, another roommate and good friend of Alina's was going to join us for the walk too. "Why aren't you guys ready yet? We are going to be late!"

Zach just smiled and shook his head. He said he had just gotten back from McDonald's and hadn't seen anyone yet. He motioned for me to come in, and I rushed up the stairs to Alina's room.

I called her name and knocked on her bedroom door, and then I turned the knob to open it. The door was locked. I knocked again, calling her name louder. No response. I wondered, "What the heck is she doing in there?" I knocked on the door harder and harder, shaking the door, calling her name louder each time.

Zach looked confused when he came up the stairs and asked me what was going on.

"I don't know what's going on! Why is she not opening the door?" That's when I realized I needed help, so I grabbed my phone and called Yan. "Yan, you need to come in here. Her door is locked, and she is not opening it." I could only hope that this was a big joke, though not a funny one.

Yan said he got chills all over his body when he heard what I said. He grabbed Benji and ran in the house. His legs were shaking as he ran up the stairs to Alina's room.

He looked scared. "Just hold Benji." He pushed the door hard. It opened, and he ran in.

I did not know what to expect, but deep inside, I hoped to find the room empty. That's when my husband screamed, "Oh my God, he killed her! Oh my God, he bashed her skull!"

I heard what was being said, but I could not process the information. It sounded so foreign. My body immediately turned to ice, and I felt a weird tingling in my head. I thought, "What the hell is he saying?"

I stepped inside and saw my daughter lying on the floor by the wall across from her bed. I screamed. I couldn't comprehend why she was lying there and why she looked the way she did. As my brain tried to make sense of the scene in front of me, all I could think was, "Is it a Halloween joke or what?"

I felt numb, like I had left my body and was watching the scene as if it were a movie. Everything was in slow motion. All I could hear was Yan screaming frantically, "Call 911... just call 911, damn it!"

I ran out of the room. All four of Alina's roommates were awakened by our screams and ran to her room, fearfully asking what had happened. All I could say was, "Her face... just call 911." Everyone was running around, screaming, confused. No one attempted to walk inside and see what was there. Benji was barking psychotically. Zach called 911. He was crying and shaking as he tried to explain the reason for his call.

A young man stepped out of Becca's bedroom, which was right across of Alina's. I didn't know who he was, but I guessed he was Becca's boyfriend. He kept asking me what was going on while Zach was calling 911 outside of Alina's room. I screamed at him "You want to know what happened?" and madly shoved him into Alina's room. I knew I had to call my son.

I ran into the kitchen, across from Alina's room. I could not breathe. I knew I had to let Artem know but was so afraid to call him. I knew that he would drive here, speeding recklessly, and I was afraid he wouldn't make it. I dialed his number. He answered quickly, "Good morning, Mom." He probably expected to be greeted with happy birthday wishes. I could not say a word. I just breathed heavily into the phone, searching for a way to minimize the shock. As calmly as possible, I just said, "Tema. You must come here. He killed her."

Not understanding what evil had befallen our family, my son immediately screamed, "What are you talking about?" I felt as if I were fainting. "Tema, he killed her," I stated, my voice shaking. "We are here in her house in Oakland, waiting for the police. Dad is going crazy. Please come here now. Please drive very carefully." But with a shaky voice, my son just kept screaming, "What are you talking about?"

I went back to Alina's room, hoping to see a different scene because I couldn't accept what I had seen before. I kept thinking, "It just can't happen." But the scene remained the same. My daughter was still lying on the floor on her back in a pool of her own blood. Yan sat on his knees next to her, holding her bleeding head. He looked pale. His hands were shaking, and he was crying.

With one hand he tried to stop a fountain of blood running out of her neck. With the other hand, he tried to wipe the blood out of her eyes, begging her to open them.

"Baby, please open your eyes," he begged. "It's ok, we'll fix everything. We'll do reconstructive surgery, and you will look perfect again. Do you hear me? Baby, please open your eyes." Then he said, "Elly, hold her hand... it's warm! And so is her tummy!" I dropped on my knees and carefully took her hand. It was a little warm. I lifted her arm so her hand could touch my face. Her arm seemed heavy though. I touched her belly, and it was a little warm too. We both prayed and hoped she would be alright.

Several minutes later, some police officers walked in and asked us to leave the room. Trusting that they would help her and keep her alive, I immediately ran outside as I had been asked. Yan did not—he refused to leave his daughter and begged the officer to tell him that she was still alive. The officer shook his head. "I'm sorry, sir, she is not. Please leave the room, and let us do our job."

My husband lost control then. He screamed hysterically that he would not leave and that he would stay with his daughter.

I ran out of the house and was met by more officers who were gathered on the porch. They asked who I was and what had happened. I could hardly breathe, but I said that I was the mother. At this point, reality had not yet hit me. I told them they could ask me any questions. I gave them Matthew Darby's name, and I told them that Alina had filed a PFA against him because he had broken into her house a few weeks ago.

After I spoke to the police officers, everything moved in slow motion. I kept repeating to myself, "No, no, no, it just could not happen." Then, I was brought back to reality when I saw my son running toward the house.

Artem was stopped by an officer at the door, who told him he could not enter. Artem became enraged, screaming that he was Alina's brother and he needed to come in. He fought and pushed everyone away, trying to get into the house. I had never seen him so angry.

I ran to him and hugged him tightly, trying to stop him from fighting. "Tema, please calm down... you have to stop, please."

My son cried and screamed and just kept asking, "Mom, what's going on?" Finally, he gained control of himself. He was pale, and I looked straight into his eyes. I sensed so much fear and agony. My son looked at me and asked, "Where is Dad?"

*   *   *

It got louder at the house as police cars, ambulances, and other trucks arrived. Suddenly, Yan appeared in the doorway of the house, carried by two police officers. My husband was unrecognizable as he screamed that he was going to kill everyone there. He cried and swore, completely out of control. He no longer had his shirt on—it had been torn or pulled off at some point while he fought the police officers who were trying to remove him from the house.

Artem and I ran to him, trying to hug and calm him down, but he was beyond consolation. He fell to his knees, hysterically punching the ground. He screamed, "Oh my God, my daughter is gone. My life is over. I am going to kill myself now."

I could not breathe. I pressed against my chest, trying to inhale, but I felt like I was choking. A group of first responders tried unsuccessfully to get Yan under control. Eventually, he was taken to an ambulance where he was sedated. They told me that he needed to be taken to a hospital, and one of the officers said that he would take Benji to his office to care for him so Artem and I could go to the hospital with Yan.

Yan was brought to the psychiatric unit of a local hospital. They ran tests and treated him with medications to stabilize him. He seemed to be getting back to normal and kept repeating, "I am okay."

I paced in the hospital room, muttering phrases of doubt and disbelief. "That just could not happen. How are we going to live with that?"

I then turned to the painful thought of the future that had just been stolen from Alina and our family. My daughter would never graduate from college. She would never be a physical therapist. Yan would never walk her down the aisle on her wedding day, and I would never hold her hand in the delivery room while she fulfilled her dream of becoming a mom.

I could not understand how this was happening, and I could not comprehend the thoughts running through my head. While trying to make sense of the chaos around me, I realized that Yan and I would have to begin a process that we never could have imagined: we had to call our family and friends to tell them our daughter was dead. I left the hospital room to begin this horrible task.

*   *   *

Although I have lived in the United States for over two decades, my family has always lived in Russia. We would visit them every two or three years, and Alina loved and cherished her Russian family. She was the only girl in the family, and she was loved and adored by my parents as well as my brothers and their families. I knew that telling them would be difficult, and I was trying to come up with the best way. I decided that my older brother would be the best person to receive such horrible news first. My brother adored his niece; he always called her "Lyal'ka," meaning "little baby doll."

I dialed his number. There, it was some time in the evening, and I was not sure if the connection would be strong enough or if my brother would answer. However, he picked up the phone in a second, and his voice was clear. I said that I had very bad news and he would need to think about how to deliver the news to our family. When I told him, my brother was shocked and said that he needed to call me back.

Next, I had to call someone from work. I immediately thought of my colleague and friend, Angie. She knew I had been planning to attend the event with my family and Benji that morning, and she had messaged me a few hours earlier saying she hoped we would have a good time, asking me to send her pictures of Benji. I dialed her number. She answered with a very cheerful voice, expecting to hear a funny story about Benji. I sighed deeply.

"Angie, Angie, Angie... I have very horrible news. He killed her." Angie knew what my daughter had been dealing with lately, so I did not have to explain. She started crying.

"Yes, Angie, he horribly, brutally murdered her. Yan and I found her in her bedroom. We are at the hospital now. I don't know what's going to happen to me next, but please let our company know I won't be at work."

She was crying and kept saying, "Oh my God, oh my God..."

*   *   *

After I had called my family and friends, I went back to the room. Yan had finished making calls to his family and friends too. My husband, my son, and I just stared at each other. We were in absolute shock and disbelief. Our world had collapsed. We were terrified and did not know what to do next.

Then, out of nowhere, our friends started popping up. They kept appearing around us, one by one, like mushrooms sprouting from the ground. Each of them had the same look: a wide-eyed, frightened face, scanning us to make sure we could function. I could not understand where all of them had come from; it was like someone waved a magic wand, and they appeared. Two detectives came to see us too. They wanted to make sure we were okay and explained what we should do next. The presence of our friends and the detectives was comforting to me; I felt so much support and compassion, and I felt that they would take care of me.

*   *   *

Finally, Yan was discharged from the hospital, and several tasks needed to be accomplished. Our friends split into groups to handle them: some went to the pharmacy to pick up our medications, some went to the grocery store, and some went to pick up Benji from the police department. I decided to drive with Artem to his house while Yan went to his mother's home to notify her.

My son drove in silence, and I was quiet too. I was still numb and in disbelief, though I didn't cry. I thought I might be in shock, and I was afraid that it could hit me at any moment and that I would lose my mind.

While we were driving, Artem got a phone call and told me we had to drive to Alina's house to pick up her hamster. We parked near the house, and I sat in the car, quietly observing the area as Artem ran back in the house. I saw people walking around the house. The police cars were still there, and now news reporters were interviewing people. The bright yellow caution tape hurt my eyes—it was everywhere. It seemed like it was wrapped around the whole sky. It looked like the crime scenes I had seen in movies, except it was real, and my daughter was the victim — I was the victim. Artem came back to the car and handed me the cage with little Snickers inside.

*　　*　　*

Snickers was Alina's sweet little hamster whom she loved and adored. We called it "Homa," which means "him." It is a boy, but Alina wanted it to be a girl. I remember laughing so hard, jokingly asking her where she had seen a girl with such a male looking under-tail. She had laughed too. "Mom, it doesn't matter. I just want it to be a girl, so it will be one regardless. Just deal with it." Every time I called Snickers "Homa," Alina always corrected me, "Mom, it's HER, not him!"

Although pets were not allowed, she secretly kept Snickers in her dorm in Greensburg, till the day I got a text from Alina, saying, "Mom, guess what... they found Homa, and she got kicked out of the house. Please come and get her." So we had to bring Homa home and take care of her. I absolutely fell in love with her; she was so cute. Every day, I reported to Alina how Homa was doing, and I constantly sent her pictures and videos of her little pet. Homa became part of the family and was best friends with

Benji. When Alina moved into her Oakland house, she took Snickers with her and kept the cage in her bedroom.

I was so glad to see Homa. I put the cage on my lap and stared at her the whole ride. She stared into my eyes the whole time and didn't move. I wished she could talk. I wished she could tell me what had happened in that room. She was the only witness. She must have seen everything.

*   *   *

I stayed at Artem's place for a while, waiting for everyone to come to our house. My daughter-in-law was speechless; she looked terrified. Her mom, who had come from Russia to visit her daughter and help take care of Angelina, had no words either. Everyone was in shock and disbelief except little Angelina, who was peacefully sleeping in her crib.

We sat in silence, wondering how things could have turned out this way. Only three weeks ago, we had all been sitting in the hospital, waiting for Angelina to enter this beautiful world. We all felt happy and excited and could not stop talking about how crazy and funny our family was, how lucky we were to have a little baby now, and how one day, Alina would bring a baby into the family too.

As we sat at Artem's now, we could not believe that the promising future we shared as a family could be destroyed in the blink of an eye and that our beautiful world could turn to ruins.

*   *   *

Yan and his friend, Henry, were on their way to Yan's mom's home. Since Yan was still shirtless, Henry had given his friend his shirt.

Yan's dad had passed away almost one year ago. It would have been exactly one year in a week, and we had planned to have a little ceremony to set up a monument at his grave. Yan's father had battled stage IV cancer for a year and a half. It had been very hard for him and tough on the family, especially Yan and his mom. Yan's parents did not speak English well, so Yan had been by their side at all times during the treatment process.

When Yan's mom opened the door, she immediately started shaking, knowing instinctively that something was wrong. Her son looked like a zombie; he was wearing a noticeably oversized shirt that was unbuttoned all the way down, and he could not stand up straight. He was being held by his friend.

"Oh my God! What happened?"

My husband cried. "I don't have a daughter anymore..."

His mom was very confused and nervously asked what he meant.

"There is no Alina anymore."

My mother-in-law started shaking and crying, not understanding what was happening. She looked at Henry, hoping to get a reasonable explanation. Henry just silently nodded, confirming that it was true.

"Mom, your granddaughter was murdered."

Then, she collapsed as if the ground had disappeared under her feet.

*   *   *

Going back to my house felt very weird. Friends and family members were gathering at our house. I did not feel like myself; I had extremely ugly emotions that I could not even define. I just knew that I absolutely hated them and wanted the day to be over. One of my friends said that I had to take medicine and shoveled a few pills into my mouth. Then I went to bed, shocked and terrified.

Chapter 2: Monday, October 9th

I woke up in the middle of the night and felt as if I had been struck by lightning or that there had been an earthquake inside my body. My heart was pounding. I immediately asked myself, "What could be wrong?" In half a second, my mind responded to me with the answer—I was not waking up *from* a nightmare; I was waking up *into* a nightmare. My mind was screaming, "No! No! No!" I was panicking. My heart hurt so much, and my breathing was very heavy. I felt as if an elephant was sitting on my chest. With everything in me, I was rejecting reality. I did not want to accept what had happened yesterday.

It was impossible for my brain to process any thoughts pertaining to yesterday's events, and the war going on inside my head kept me awake. Yan was not sleeping either. The difference was that his brain *did* process what had happened yesterday, and he was terrified that he would have flashbacks if he went to sleep. He was terrified of how he had last seen Alina's face and what had been done to it. He could not get the image out of his mind — that horrifying picture kept appearing in front of his eyes so clearly. That was one of the most terrifying nights of our lives, and we knew it would be followed by so many more. We knew we would have to get up in the morning and start making funeral arrangements for our daughter.

*　　*　　*

Yan's mom and two of our good friends, Lusy and Igor, stayed overnight at our house. I had called Lusy when I was waiting at Artem's house. She and Igor lived in Cleveland, and they were having a good time on their boat exploring Lake Erie when I had called. Our conversation was very short. I simply stated what had happened to our daughter and told them that I would let them know all the details later. A few hours later, Lusy and Igor were in our house.

The five of us gathered in the kitchen in the early morning. Lusy took care of everything, including cooking, cleaning, and making sure we were eating when we had absolutely no desire to do so. Our friends and families gathered at our house again. I was still numb. Thinking about going to a funeral home for my daughter was making me sick. My mind was fighting that unimaginable thought, so I was on autopilot.

We decided to go to the same funeral home where Yan's father had been taken care of only a year ago. Since they knew our family already, we thought it would bring us some comfort. We were greeted by the manager, Mike, at the front door. Mike was very nice and polite, and of course he immediately recognized our faces. As we followed Mike through the building, I knew exactly what room he was taking us to. Everything looked familiar; I just could not believe that I was there for my daughter now. That could not be real. The image of my young and beautiful daughter who was full of life and energy just could not be associated with this place.

Mike expressed his deepest condolences for our daughter and began his normal routine. He went through a list of services to see which ones we wanted to use. None of his words made sense to me. I felt like they were reaching my brain, but instead of being processed, they were bouncing back. Then we were asked to do something that no parent should ever be asked to do. Mike asked us to choose a casket for our daughter.

Yan, Artem, and I quietly followed Mike to the casket storage room. He gently opened the door for us, saying that we could walk in whenever we were ready. Then he left us alone. My body was paralyzed. I was not able to cross over the threshold. Yan made the first move, and then my son put his arm around me, helping me proceed. We all were shaking, looking around and trying to see what we liked the most. "This is insane," I thought. Then, I told my husband and son that I wanted the most beautiful casket for our daughter. I nervously glanced from one casket to another. Then my eyes met Yan's. I saw so much desperation in them. Then, we both were crying. "Oh my God, what are we doing?!"

Artem was not doing well emotionally either. He hugged us both, saying that we had to be strong, and despite our devastation, we must finish the process. For a few minutes we stood in a circle, hugging each other, trying to calm down. I felt as if we were hugging so tightly while sharing our unbearable pain that we became one.

"There have always been four of us," Yan finally said, "and there will still be four of us no matter what. Okay, guys, let's pick a new home for our girl now." And the coffin we chose for Alina was beautiful.

The last thing we had to do was drive to the cemetery and choose a lot. To our surprise, an open spot was right across from my father-in-law's grave. We could not believe it. A little orange flag marked the spot.

I dropped to my knees. I touched the ground, crying, "Oh my God, my poor child is going to be lying here . . . I don't want it to be like this!" My soul was screaming. I could not believe this was happening. Then I looked back and saw the headstone with my father-in-law's face just a few steps away. It gave me some comfort, and I thought, "At least she will not have to be afraid of being here alone. Her grandpa will be right next to her."

I remembered how Alina had stood at her grandpa's grave. Every time, she would tell me how beautiful and peaceful it was and how pretty the tree was that stood right across from her grandpa. I will never forget saying to her, "Alina, can you imagine being buried under that beautiful tree? The best view ever!" She smiled and said, "I know . . . Whoever takes this spot would be so lucky." Who would have known that a few months later, that beautiful spot would be taken, and the "lucky" person would be my daughter?

After the funeral arrangements were done, we went home. Our friends continued to help and comfort us by expressing their love and compassion. Our good friend, Ghena, walked in the house with a huge portrait of Alina. We were going to place it next to her casket at the viewing. My heart almost stopped when I saw the portrait. It was one of Alina's high school senior pictures. She looked stunning. She was not smiling in that picture, and her big, beautiful, brown eyes were staring at me, screaming, "Mom, how come?" I could not understand "how come." How come the most beautiful picture of my daughter, one that had always mesmerized me when I looked at it, had become her memorial portrait?

Yan put the portrait on a stand, blocking the TV screen. Our beautiful child was silently looking at us. Her face looked very cold and sad. I kept hearing her, "How come, Mom? How come?"

*   *   *

"Elly, we need to go buy a dress for her," Yan's mom said. I panicked. How could a mother go shopping for that type of dress?

I always pictured myself shopping with Alina for her wedding dress one day. She already knew the style and design she would choose, and she could not wait to be a happy, beautiful bride walking down the aisle, her loving father holding her hand. But instead, I had to go pick a dress for her to wear in her coffin. My mind raced. I kept thinking, "My beautiful daughter is going to wear her beautiful dress lying in her beautiful casket!" The task of choosing the dress was too much for me, and I just could not do it. Kate and Lusy offered their help, and trusting them with such an important but very painful mission, I let them choose the last dress my daughter would ever wear.

Chapter 3: Tuesday, October 10th

I woke up in the middle of the night with the same feeling as the night before: storms raging in my body, lightning and earthquakes jolting me awake. My heart was pounding, and millions of terrifying thoughts were racing through my mind. I felt panicked, like an atomic bomb had been dropped on our family. Yan felt the same. We tried to calm ourselves, but nothing could stop or relieve our fear and agony. We just wanted this scary night to be over, but we also knew that when it ended and daylight came, we would be going to our daughter's viewing.

The thought of having a viewing for my daughter made me feel unhinged. "A viewing? For Alina? No. No. No. This just cannot be real!" For the first time in my life, as I tried to fall asleep, I wished that I would never wake up.

*　　*　　*

I must have fallen asleep because, to my dismay, I did wake up. I felt like a zombie. I was on autopilot, and I started my morning routine. All I could think was, "What does my daughter look like right now?" I could not stop that thought, and I did not want to believe that my daughter was in a casket.

My family parked at the funeral home. Once again, I felt terrified. Mike greeted us at the front door and said that they had done an amazing job fixing our daughter's face and making her look good. He said we would be surprised. Yan and I wanted to see her first before the others joined us. Mike opened the door to the chapel where the ceremonies took place. Holding each other, my husband and I slowly walked down the aisle, approaching the closed casket. My legs were shaking, and I had a hard time making them take each step. We made it all the way down, and here was *the casket.* We were both crying and touching it in disbelief of what we were doing.

When we told Mike we were ready for him to open it, I felt like I was going to faint. We stepped outside of the area where the casket stood, and Mike closed the curtains that separated this special area from the public space. We nervously waited. In a couple of minutes, the curtains were opened, and Mike left the room to give us some privacy with our daughter.

That was it. The casket was open. Yan started screaming and crying aloud, looking at his daughter, "Oh my God, baby, oh my God, my poor little girl! How could that have happened to you?" I stared at the casket in a state of complete shock. I was not seeing my daughter in that casket. I felt like I was looking at a wax figure of some old lady whose face I could not recognize.

I screamed hysterically, "Yan, that is not Alina! Oh my God, that's not our daughter!" I was going mad, trying to figure out where Alina could be if it was not her lying in the casket. I felt that I was truly losing my mind.

Yan tried to calm me down; he held me tightly, repeating, "Elly, listen to me . . . that *is* our daughter. Baby, that *is* our Alina.

That's her. We've lost her." But I refused to believe what he said to me. I felt like a cold statue with no feelings or emotions. I was completely numb.

Yan touched her hair. "Elly, please get closer. This is Alina's hair." I moved closer to her head, so I was looking at her body from a different angle. I could not see her face then. With only the top of her head in my view, I touched her dark wavy hair and started crying, "Oh my God, it does feel like Alina's hair." Then, I held her head, looking for the wound, hoping not to find any. But it was there. The stitched wound with dried blood was there. I started shaking and howling, "Oh my God, Yan, that's where he hit her! Oh my God, it must have hurt her so bad!"

In that moment, all those scary emotions poured over me again. I felt my daughter's pain and how scared she must have been. "Oh my God, Yan, that *is* our Alina! That *is* her beautiful hair! It smells like her hair, and I do recognize her cute little forehead!" We both cried. I wanted to hold her hand, but it was very heavy and cold as ice. I felt like I was leaving my body. I was getting numb again. It was time to call our family into the room.

*   *   *

Meeting Alina for the first time in her new form was extremely painful and devastating for everyone in the family. We gave everyone their time with her, and then the casket was closed. We wanted our beautiful daughter to be remembered by everyone else the way she was when she was alive.

The viewing started. People came in to say "goodbye" to our daughter. I sat in a chair next to my daughter's coffin, and I had a hard time comprehending that such an event was really happening. I think my soul was pushed out of my body so it would not be destroyed from such excruciating pain. One by one, people expressed their condolences, hugging and saying "sorry." I had switched back to autopilot, and I said "thank you," trying to smile at everyone to show my appreciation for their attendance. I felt completely numb and was curious why I was not crying.

Yan could not stop his tears. This made me mad because I saw my husband as a strong person, and at that moment, I felt like he was not. Everyone cried except me. The line of people was never-ending, and I could not wait for the viewing to be over. I just wanted everyone to leave so I could go back home where everything would go back to normal again. My mind refused to accept anything that was happening, and I just wanted this horror movie to end.

Chapter 4: Wednesday, October 11th

The next day, I sat by the closed casket of my daughter again. I felt numb, paralyzed, and in total disbelief of what was happening. People came in for the second viewing. And again, one by one, they were hugging and saying how sorry they were. Some of them had come for a second time. The line seemed to be even longer than it had been yesterday. Alina's friends, family, teachers, doctors, and people from her high school, work, university, some of whom I was seeing for the first time, flooded the room. It seemed that the whole city of Pittsburgh had come to express their condolences to our family and say "goodbye" to our daughter.

In the middle of the viewing, Yan came up to me and said we needed to go to another room because the detectives were waiting for us there. Detective David and Detective Chuck were very kind and compassionate. They both hugged me, expressing their sympathy, and informed us that they had good news. They said that their investigation had been successful — they were aware of Darby's location, and they would have him by the end of the day. I appreciated their help and hard work, but at the same time, I realized that I didn't care at that moment. I had completely forgotten about Darby. I had forgotten that he had run away and that the police had been searching for him. All I could think about was my beautiful daughter lying in that closed casket while my mind was screaming, "No. No. No. This cannot be true."

The chapel filled with mourners. People took their seats, waiting for the service to begin. Since my family had never practiced any religion, Sarah, the cantor at the funeral home, agreed to do a formal but general ceremony. Sarah did an amazing job giving words to something that was unspeakable. She said such beautiful things about Alina and her happy, beautiful life. Throughout the ceremony, I stared at my daughter's portrait sitting in front of her casket. I didn't blink, and I felt like I was not breathing either. I looked straight into her beautiful brown eyes. They screamed at me with such horror, "How come, Mom? How come?"

Our family and friends were invited to speak in remembrance of Alina. It was heart-wrenching to listen. When my son's name was called so he could share his words about his sister, I felt like his name was echoing. Here was my son, standing in front of me. My firstborn child, my handsome young man who had just started his adult life as a happy husband and father. That was my boy up there, standing next to a closed casket containing his baby sister. The sister with whom he had shared his life for twenty years. That lovely little girl who had always felt so proud of her big brother. Both of my children appeared in front of me; my daughter in a casket with her beautiful eyes screaming from the portrait and my son wearing an unfamiliar face, a face of agony and horror. I was paralyzed looking at my children. The voice inside of my head kept screaming, "This just *cannot* be real." And then, Artem spoke.

"A few days ago, I was supposed to be waking up to celebrate my 25th birthday. Instead, I woke up to a complete nightmare." He paused between tears and then described the horror that overcame him when he received my phone call informing him of his sister's death. "I never drove so fast in my life."

He was very emotional; his voice was shaking. I was shaking too. I could hear people crying everywhere in the chapel.

"My sister had such a lovable nature, an ambitious drive to become a physical therapist, and the ability to uplift friends and family with her sense of humor and fun-loving, charismatic personality. She excelled at singing, dancing, and gymnastics and had a love for animals and children. When my daughter, Angelina, was born over the summer, Alina was by my side. I could keep talking for days about what a great person and loving sister Alina was.

"Every time I look into my daughter's eyes, I will think God put Alina's soul inside of her." At this statement, my body shook with chills. Finally, I started to cry.

Yan's cousin, Paul, was the next person to share his words. Paul and Alina had had a special bond. They could talk forever about different subjects and events in which they shared a common interest. At every family gathering, she would sit next to Paul at the table. The majority of our family spoke exclusively Russian at the table, but Paul was proficient in both Russian and English. Since Alina did not feel comfortable having her conversations in Russian, she preferred sitting next to Paul and chatting with him in English. She enjoyed their conversations so much, always laughing and sharing her thoughts about the world from a new generation's point of view. When I would try to chime in with my opinion about their topic of discussion, she always laughed, responding, "Mom, you are an old generation!"

Paul took a moment to gain his composure before talking about his niece. He described how Alina's eyes resembled her father's. "We always used to make fun of how she was a Daddy's girl and looked just like him." He went on about how much Alina loved life, and then he made an appeal to the investigators. "To all the detectives, to the city, this is not your ordinary case. We demand justice!"

After Paul spoke, a young man took his spot next to Alina's casket. His face was familiar to me, and I realized he must have been one of Alina's high school friends. He introduced himself as "Salvatore." One of Alina's old pictures immediately popped up in my head in that moment — it was one of her prom pictures. She was in her beautiful long red dress next to a boy in a white suit with a bright red tie that complemented Alina's dress. The two of them looked absolutely adorable together, happy and smiling. I remembered looking at that picture and asking Alina who that cute guy next to her was and joking that he should have been her prom date. I remembered her making a cute, silly grimace, then shrieking, "Ha-ha! It's Sal! And he is just my good friend."

Sal expressed his condolences and said that families should never go through this. He talked about how beautiful and smart Alina was. "She was too perfect for this world; God wanted her back." All my insides started protesting. My mind was screaming, "Oh my God, what is that supposed to mean... she was too perfect for this world? My daughter was just perfect for me, perfect for her dad, perfect for her family and friends, so perfect for this world that she loved so much! She was meant to be a part of this wonderful world and never disappear!" At the time, I didn't understand what he meant.

*   *   *

Toward the end of the service, Sarah sang the song "Memory" from one of Alina's favorite musicals, *Cats*.

41

Memory

All alone in the moonlight

I can dream of the old days

Life was beautiful then

I remember the time I knew what happiness was

Let the memory live again.

Sarah's voice was beautiful. At this point, I was sobbing, remembering Alina singing this bittersweet ballad. I remembered how beautiful she looked on stage when she played Grizabella, the Glamour Cat, at one of her dance school shows. The whole audience had cried. That number was one of Alina's best performances. People had been touched to the core by her beautiful and heartfelt singing. And now that audience was watching a different scene. A scene that they had never expected Alina to be a part of. The scene where a breathless "Grizabella" was leaving a real stage called life and becoming just a memory. The whole audience was crying again. Crying and whispering, "Let the memory live again."

*   *   *

Then, the pallbearers were called. I watched as six men approached my daughter's casket and lined both sides, getting ready to carry my daughter away. Away from me forever. My body felt a strong desire to shut down. Without blinking, I stared at the cold, agonized faces of these six men and realized they were six of our best friends. Our friends who had watched our daughter grow up and become the beautiful young lady she was. Our friends with whom we had spent so much time as a family. Six fathers whose daughters were like sisters to Alina, growing up together, celebrating holidays and birthday parties, going on vacations and fun trips together. These six fathers never imagined that they would be part of such an unimaginable event. An event where they would be carrying the casket containing the lifeless body of a child. A child who had been a daughter of their best friends. Now they were taking their best friends' daughter on her last trip. The trip that would forever take her away from her loving parents and the beautiful world in which they had existed together.

My beautiful child was carried away from my sight. The portrait of my daughter was all we had left. Her big, beautiful brown eyes were still looking at me. They never stopped screaming, "How come, Mom? How come?"

As we headed to the cemetery, I became completely numb again. I stood quietly at the open grave, watching my daughter's casket slowly descend to the very bottom. Watching her take her final journey, knowing I would never see her prance down the stairs, humming her favorite songs. Knowing I would never get another call, another text, another Facebook message from her containing some cute story or one of the adorable animal videos we often exchanged. Knowing that the person with whom I shared all of my silliness and happiness was being buried in front of me and wondering if those qualities of mine would be buried with her.

I willed her to throw open the casket and sit up. I willed her to scream at me and her father to ask what the hell we were doing and why the hell she was in a casket. Instead, the casket was lowered fully into the ground. It was too much to bear. I held Kate's arm, leaning on her with the whole weight of my body. I couldn't feel my legs, and I had a hard time accepting that this scene was real. I felt like I had left my body again and was watching the scene from the outside just as I had felt in her bedroom when we found her body.

I was in complete shock and disbelief, unable to comprehend that the open grave was engulfing the body of my own daughter, and I felt distracted seeing Yan kneeling down at the edge of the grave and loudly crying. I got cold chills and tingling all over my body. Suddenly, a rancid scent awoke me. One of our friends, a doctor, held smelling salts to my face because I had fainted. I was back, and it was time to say goodbye.

One by one, people walked to the edge of the grave and dropped a pinch of soil on top of Alina's casket. The soil fell for what seemed like forever, finding its home deep in the ground. Mother Earth had my daughter now. This casket was Alina's new home.

*   *   *

After the cemetery, people gathered at our house. I was confused and tired—physically and emotionally. It was loud, and the presence of so many people and the transition of their talking into laughing annoyed me. I could not stop thinking about tomorrow. "What is tomorrow going to look like? How are we going to live without Alina?" I had no desire to talk to anyone. I didn't want to eat; I didn't want to drink. I just wanted to be alone. I was so overwhelmed with all these ugly feelings that my body needed to recharge. I needed to shut myself down. I went upstairs and waited for everyone to leave.

My family in Russia was devastated when they had found out what happened. My older brother had delivered the horrible news to our younger brother and our dad. They did not know how to tell our mom. When they did, my mom didn't take the news well. She could not comprehend that Alina was gone. She could not comprehend that her sweet granddaughter, whom she had been holding in her arms just a few months ago, had been killed. She had a hard time comprehending that Alina had not just been killed in a car crash or had lost her life due to some accident but that her sweet little girl had been murdered. In shock and disbelief, she just kept asking my dad and her sons what they meant by saying that. I remember my sister-in-law calling me after hearing the news. Her voice was shaking, and she cried, repeating my name, "Elly. Elly." I didn't know what to say to her either. I remember whispering, "I don't know, I don't know." My family was not able to come to the funeral and be by my side because it's very complicated for Russian citizens to get visas in such a short period of time and come to the United States. My family felt devastated and helpless.

I needed to call my mom to see how she was doing. It was nighttime in Russia when I called, but my mom was not sleeping, she was waiting for me to call. My voice was very cold, and I didn't cry. I just simply told her how the funeral had gone and that I didn't know how I was going to live now. My mom didn't say much either. She was scared that I was suicidal and might harm myself.

One by one, people left. As they left, they shared nice, heartfelt words while kissing and hugging us and offering their help at any time. Despite the presence of ugliness and devastation inside of my body, I was touched by their love and compassion. It was a blessing to have so many loving and supportive people by our side.

Everyone left, and our house was silent. Alina was gone. All we had left was the large portrait hanging on a wall in the living room. Her big, beautiful eyes were still looking at me, but they had stopped screaming. Now, they were piteously whispering, "How come, Mom? How come?"

PART II: AFTER

Chapter 5: Returning to Work

After missing work for a week, both Yan and I felt it was time to return. I am an accountant and work in the finance department of a well-known insurance agency. Yan is an engineer at a large mining company. No one expected us to return to work so soon, but we both felt that we absolutely had to get out of the house and be among other people; otherwise we both would lose our minds.

I was not able to drive myself, so Yan drove me to work early in the morning. I felt weird and out of place coming into my office and turning on my computer. I knew I had to face my co-workers with my new status—bereaved mother—a status that no parent ever thinks they will attain. Just one week before, I had been a happy and proud mother, and now, I would be branded as the employee whose daughter was brutally murdered. My "title" had been forever changed.

I felt so much pain, anger, disappointment, and surprisingly, shame. Some unexplainable type of embarrassment made me feel very awkward. I did not feel like myself anymore. I felt like I had lost my identity and that the people at work would judge me. I felt like a failure of a mother, one who had allowed her daughter to be taken in such an unimaginable way. I felt very guilty for being unable to save my child's life, but I fought these feelings aggressively. My mind was spinning, screaming inside, "No, my daughter is the best daughter. She always has been. And I'm a good mother. I can't be that loser parent who has just lost her child; my child cannot be lost." Even if these feelings were not rational, they were very real to me.

Two of my close friends at work, Angie and Anastasia, came into my office to check on how I was adapting to my new role as a grieving mother. They let me vent until I could no longer speak. They were very supportive and compassionate. Then, other people popped into my office to express their sympathy. I put a mask on and tried hard to seem as normal as possible. I was touched by their attention, but I felt very weird. It was so hard to look into people's eyes. At some point, I felt as if I was some type of weird, exotic animal in a zoo, and people only came to see me because of their curiosity of what the mother of a murdered child looked like. How does someone look when their entire world has been ripped out from under them? The first thing some people said after looking at me was, "Aww, you look good." And I felt as if I was disappointing them. Like I hadn't met their expectations of how the face of true misery should appear. I felt that they expected to see something horribly weird and ugly.

The atmosphere was intense. People just didn't know what to say and offered those common phrases that were "supposed" to be said to people experiencing loss. I appreciated their compassion, but none of their words sounded right to me. None of them. In fact, some of these words of "compassion" were extremely painful.

Someone: "She is in a better place now."

My mind: What better place? Her best place was here next to me. She loved that place so much, and there is no better place than that.

Someone: "She is still here with you."

My mind: Where? Do you see her? Is she really here with me? Don't you see she is not? Your child is still with you, alive and happy, so just try to pretend your own child is gone and be ok at thinking he is still with you when you *know* he is not.

Someone: "It will get better; it takes time."

My mind: How can it get better? My daughter is gone! What takes time? Waiting for her to come back? She will never come back, so it will take me a lifetime to get better. It will not get better until I join her.

Someone: "Something good will come out of this."

My mind: Oh my God, how dare you think the brutal murder of my poor child would bring something good into my life? My child is dead, my heart is forever broken, my family is destroyed, and nothing will ever be good anymore!

Someone: "You're so young... you have to live."

My mind: My daughter was only 20! So you really think it was OK for HER to die?

Someone: "You have to live for your family; they love you."

My mind: I never planned to stop loving my family, and I will never stop living for them, but my daughter is gone! My daughter is part of my family, and she isn't living anymore.

Someone: "At least you have your son and your granddaughter."

My mind: Oh my God! Having only one of my two children is not a gift. Could you choose which one of your kids you would prefer to let go of and which one to keep? Even if I had ten other kids, it would not make me feel any better. I do not love my children in parts. I love both with my whole heart. Without one, my whole heart is damaged.

Someone: "At least she was not living with you for the last two years, so it's easier for you now."

My mind: How stupid to think that I loved my child less because she was living in a different house. She was living in my heart no matter where she was located. If anything, perhaps my pain was worsened by the fact that we did not spend every moment of her last days together.

Someone: "I know. I understand."

My mind: How do you know? Have you lost your child too? You don't understand anything.

I wanted to scream about how rude and heartless those words sounded to me, but I just said a short "thank you" to people. I knew they were saying something positive to make me feel better somehow, but there was nothing that could take my pain away. There was nothing to stop my heart, now broken into a million pieces, from bleeding. I knew nothing would ever fix the fact that my daughter was gone forever. It was as if I had been breathing life through my daughter, and now that she was gone, I was not able to breathe. I felt suffocated. As a normal human being, I had always been afraid of dying. Now I was afraid of living.

* * *

It was very tough to be at work every day, but it helped both of us stay grounded and keep going. Some days I felt I could not handle staying home at all, and it felt better to be with my colleagues at the office. My friends at work literally saved my life by offering their love, support, companionship, and understanding while I was adapting to a life of grief, which, before this tragedy, was foreign to me. They not only let me share my grief with them and helped to lighten its heavy burden by taking some of it onto themselves, but they also patiently listened to every single word I said. I had to release my sadness, my anger, my disappointment, and they patiently listened and helped me process my emotions by allowing me to express them. They didn't give advice. They didn't judge my actions or my words. They just let me grow and develop into the "new me"—the new, broken, devastated, forever changed me. They made me feel normal when I was far from it. I was now abnormal, but being abnormal became my new normal.

Yan's company had shown great support to him too. We were so lucky to be surrounded by such compassionate and supportive people at work.

Chapter 6: Grief Counseling

Living each day of our new life was like riding a roller coaster. My daughter and what had happened to her were on my mind every single second of every single minute of every single hour of every single day. No matter what I was doing or talking about, the thought of Alina ran parallel. Every action hurt. Every topic of conversation hurt.

I felt so much guilt for doing simple things because she could not do them anymore. There was a voice in my head that never stopped talking to me, questioning me. *How could I eat if she couldn't eat?* She loved pizza and chocolate milk so much. *How could I walk outside and enjoy the fresh air if she couldn't?* Her legs didn't work anymore, and she was no longer breathing. *How could I enjoy playing with Angelina if Alina couldn't hold her and laugh with her?* I knew she had loved that little girl so much and wanted to enjoy spending time with her. *How could I go holiday shopping and buy things for others if Alina wouldn't get anything anymore?* I just loved making her happy by giving her presents and watching her get excited.

Every single action felt devastating. It made me pity my child, who had been deprived of everything. To continue living my life felt as if I was betraying my poor daughter. Seeing other people go on with their lives was heartbreaking. Why were they still walking, breathing, laughing, and doing day-to-day things, and my daughter was just kicked out of the world? And for what reason? She loved life more than anyone. She did not deserve to be destroyed. She had a good life plan and was succeeding in reaching all her goals. She was smart, unique, talented, kind, beautiful, and loving. She never wanted to leave this world early—in fact, she was passionate about making it a better place.

I was angry and disappointed with life.

I realized that life was not what I always thought it was. These feelings were beyond my comprehension. I didn't see logic in life anymore, and I had completely lost my purpose. I couldn't identify a single reason to keep living this life. The whole world had collapsed, and I hated everything around me. There was a huge hole inside of me, such an empty feeling that I had never experienced before. I was unable to describe that emptiness to others because it couldn't be described in words; it was so intense that it would speak to you in the very language of your soul.

I was scared. Scared to accept the fact that Alina was gone. Scared to accept the fact that I had to keep going without her. The beautiful world had turned into ruins. And I didn't want to exist in it anymore.

I knew I needed help. Neither Yan nor I had ever participated in counseling, so I had no idea what counselors did to make people feel better. I knew it would not be the same kind of treatment I got at my regular doctor. It was not as if I just had a headache, which a doctor could easily diagnose and treat. I was very skeptical about therapy. I knew that no medication could ever heal me. Bringing my daughter back would be the only treatment to heal my broken heart. Regardless, I decided to give it a try, thinking, "Maybe counseling does some magic." Yan supported me in my decision to try the "magic" of therapy.

Wendy, our grief counselor, is a kind woman. She was recommended to me as a highly rated, experienced counselor. I felt very comfortable talking to her, and it felt like I could talk forever, but it was not what I needed. There was no magic. Yan and I shared our feelings during our sessions, but it was not helping at all. At some point, it made me feel even worse. I got frustrated listening to Yan's story. He said things I didn't want to hear, and it made me mad. He seemed very weak in those moments, and I had always admired his strength, allowing him to lead me through life.

Previously, Yan had been a major in the Russian Army for fifteen years. My husband had always been a role model for his kids, showing them strength and discipline. My kids and I had always felt safe and secure, knowing that he would take care of us. I was just not ready to see his transformation — from a brave officer to a crying, suffering man. I guess I was expecting him to help me, but he was in pain himself and was grieving too. I never expected him to grieve that hard, and I guess I was just not prepared for it or for any of what we went through.

During our sessions, Yan would beat himself up for being such an irresponsible father. He took all the blame on himself. He would cry and tell Wendy that he should have handled things differently and that if he had been a better father, Alina would still be here with us. I could not listen to any of this talk because his words caused me to hurt even more. I knew he was the most caring and loving dad. He was always there for his son and his daddy's girl. When she turned sixteen, Alina was in no hurry to get her driver's license because her daddy would drive her any place she wanted to go and would help her with anything she needed. It seemed like Yan's number was like a 9-1-1 call for them; every time they needed help or just sought advice, they knew they could simply call Daddy, and he would be right there for them. I knew he was the perfect father for his kids, and yet he sat there and cried, expressing the devastating guilt of being an irresponsible parent.

After a couple of sessions, we decided to see our counselor individually. I felt better talking to her privately. But still, talking was not helping me. I did so much talking with my girlfriends at work; they let me talk and just listened. Wendy, however, would not just listen; she gave me the advice that I needed but was not yet ready to hear. What she told me made me mad.

She said that I was in a "denial stage," and I had to open myself up and let the grief and pain go through me. She said that I should accept the fact that Alina was physically gone but that she would stay with me in my heart forever. All my insides were protesting that advice. I felt very stubborn. I was freaking out, thinking about how much more pain she wanted me to feel. I could hardly bear what I had already felt. Her words that Alina would "always be in my heart" pissed me off. I thought that if that was the only option I had, then this was all bullshit. My daughter had always been in my heart, and she would have stayed in my heart no matter what. But she was gone, and I desperately needed her back. I was not ready to face the reality that my counselor presented.

I realized that with all her experience and professionalism Wendy was not able to perform magic. She could not bring my daughter back. I stopped scheduling sessions with her. Over time, she checked up on me and reminded me that she was still willing to help with anything. I was touched by her compassion and willingness, but my response remained, "Thank you, but I am ok." That was my standard response to everyone, but not even I believed it.

Chapter 7: Facing the Reality

Yan did not feel that he needed any more counseling sessions either. He never denied that his daughter was gone. He accepted the reality. It was absolutely clear to him. His brain had processed and registered that horrific event, and he was now dealing with all the painful emotions that his mind and his body were producing in response to that upsetting thought. He cried a lot. Yan spent much of his workday driving, so he had a lot of time alone where he could relieve his emotions and let his tears flow.

In contrast, my brain still could not process what had happened. I simply didn't want to accept it, so my brain just rejected it. I felt numb often. Sometimes I felt that my mind was playing tricks on me, pretending that everything was okay like nothing had happened. I would get very confused then, thinking that I should not feel like nothing had happened because I knew the reality was quite different. I didn't cry. I just wanted my life to be the way it was before. I knew Alina was dead, but I so desperately did not want her to be. I continued to feel like I was going crazy. I had never felt so angry in my life.

Nights were the worst. The flashbacks from that day and the terrifying thoughts about what might have happened in Alina's room that night were agonizing. My mind replayed that scene over and over. My heart physically hurt. Yan experienced the same pain. We were both scared to go to bed. For the first few months, we would take a small dose of diazepam to help us sleep, but it did not do much. Every single night was an absolute nightmare for us, filled with "what ifs" and "should haves." These thoughts were driving us mad.

Every morning, we felt as though we were waking up on the same day. Trapped on October 8th. Our daughter was being murdered every single night, and we were finding her every single morning. For a moment after opening my eyes in the morning, I would optimistically think that it all must have been a nightmare, and I would feel glad that I had finally woken from it. Then, it would hit me so hard when I realized that it was real—my daughter was dead. That short second of relief was immediately transformed into a horrifying, everlasting panic attack.

Getting up and starting each day felt absolutely impossible. Every single morning Yan would drag me out of bed and convince me to get dressed. He would feed me breakfast and drive me to work. Trying to seem normal in public took so much energy. I could only function until lunch time. The rest of the day I spent feeling as if I'd died, but they had forgotten to bury me.

Chapter 8: Alina's Room

We knew that we had to go to Alina's house one day and empty her room. I also knew that there was no way I could enter that house again. I remembered how excited Alina had been about moving into her new home in Oakland.

Alina and four of her friends signed a lease agreement to rent a big three-story house with five bedrooms. They could not wait to live there as a "college family." Alina was the lucky one who got the biggest bedroom, which was located on the second floor. She was very happy decorating her room and setting everything up. Yan had worked hard to put in new carpet and had done a good job. We bought a very pretty comforter for her bed and matching curtains for her window. She hung a huge Russian flag above her desk and a big towel with a Russian nesting doll on another wall. She was so proud of her Russian heritage.

The day after we moved her in, she sent me a video of how everything was set up in her bedroom. She started the video showing the entrance door, followed by a rack of what looked like a thousand shoes. Then she panned the camera to her pretty, comfy bed, then to her nightstand, which held a little icon of the Mother of God we had gotten in Russia on our last trip there. The room was clean and very organized. Her closet was filled with hundreds of articles of clothing, which looked amazing.

Everything was just beautiful and perfect. She was so excited for her new life as a responsible adult and could not wait to take care of her new home.

Little did she know that her new life in her new home would only last for two months. Two months of texting, "Mom, I just left." "Mom, I am home now." "Mom, look what I am cooking." "Mom, can you bring Benji? I miss him so much." Two short months of a happy and fun life in crowded, noisy Oakland that she enjoyed so much where we had loved visiting her house and spending time with her in her cozy room.

After she was gone, we kept pushing that visit aside until we were ready. I also knew that I would never be ready. How could you re-enter the room where you had personally discovered your destroyed child? I would get sick from even hearing the word "Oakland."

Right before Thanksgiving, the landlord called. He was very sorry, but he had to ask us to empty Alina's room. I refused to go. Yan was offered help from his friends, but he wanted his privacy with such an emotional task. Artem said he would help. I had no idea what to do with her things. My mind spun as I tried to reconcile what kind of visit Yan would have at our daughter's house this time. Nothing felt real. I could not picture him coming back home with all her belongings. Just her things and not Alina herself.

Yan had finally picked a day for his trip, a trip that no father should ever make. It was on Thanksgiving Day. On that happy day when all families get together and express their love to each other, my husband was going to re-enter his daughter's room.

My feeling of anxiety and anticipation was at its highest level. But just the day before the trip, I got a very strong feeling that I needed to go too. Despite my fear and pain, I decided to go with

Yan. I knew I was going to the place where my daughter had taken her last breath, and I desperately wanted to feel her presence.

Early on Thanksgiving morning, Yan and I parked in Oakland. Mr. Sciulli, the landlord, was waiting for us on the front porch of his house. The house belonged to his big Italian family. It had so many family memories that he treasured. He had taken good care of that house and had been leasing it to college students for years.

Mr. Sciulli looked devastated. He gave us a hug and apologized for everything. He said we could take as much time as we needed before entering the house. Then he left, giving us some privacy.

I walked in first, and Yan followed me. The fog and numbness immediately kicked in. I told myself, "No, no, I can't get numb. I want to feel my daughter." I walked slowly up the steps, trying to focus on myself so I wouldn't get disconnected. And here was the door. The door that Alina's video had begun with. The happy door that Alina had proudly opened a few months ago to enter her beautiful room in her new life. The scary door that Yan and I had broken down to enter a much different world. The evil world we got pushed into without being given a choice to ever escape from. Here was that door. The door that had made us prisoners of our new life.

I walked in. I knew exactly where I would look first. The wall on the right side of the door. The splashes of blood were all over that wall. Then I looked down. A piece of carpet was missing. A piece the size of my daughter had been cut out. I sat on her bed. I was in as much shock as I was that very day. I stared at the shoe rack, remembering how she had been lying right next to it. The shoes were covered with blood. I sat quietly without moving, trying to process what exactly had happened in that room. And then it hit me. I started to really *feel* what had happened in that room. The pain and emotions could not be described. I lay on her pillow where I could smell her scent. I cried, "My poor child, my poor girl."

Yan walked into the room. He cried. He asked if I was ready to pack up her stuff. I panicked, saying that we couldn't bring her stuff home. These things were hers. And if she had left, she needed all her things with her. Yan gave me a bag, and one by one I put her shoes in there. I tried to clean off the blood. I pressed every shoe to my chest, then to my face before putting it into the bag. Then I emptied her closet. One by one, I placed her beautiful clothes in the bag.

Bringing my daughter's clothes back to our house didn't feel right. I didn't want Alina's clothes to belong to anyone. I wanted to put all of her shoes and clothes in the big dumpster next to her house. That was the only thing that felt right in that moment.

Yan said he would do whatever I wanted, and before taking all the bags outside, he asked one more time if I really wanted to get rid of these things. I was overwhelmed, I felt devastated, and I could not do what I was doing anymore. I panicked, saying that Alina needed her things with her. Period. I thought, if she was gone, her clothes should be gone too. I felt as if my daughter wanted to take all her things with her, but later, I regretted that decision. I wish I had kept all her shoes and clothes.

I took her purse and personal belongings with me; I wanted to put them in her room in our house. The icon of the Mother of God was one of them. I held it, screaming at God for not protecting my child.

Artem showed up when we had already packed everything. He looked so lost. He stood in the middle of the room observing every corner, trying to process what had happened that night. He had never been given a chance to enter the room that day.

Artem helped Yan carry out the heavy things and empty the room. That was it. Our daughter was nowhere to be found.

Chapter 9: Saying Goodbye

Yan and I drove away from Oakland. With everything I had, I felt that my daughter was gone. The thought that she was never coming back hit me so hard. I felt indescribably terrified.

We wanted to visit Alina's grave to wish her a Happy Thanksgiving and tell her that we had cleaned her room so she could have all her shoes and clothes with her now.

Yan needed to go to the bank first. We parked in the PNC parking lot. Yan left me alone with myself. I stared at Alina's picture that Yan had put in the front panel of his car. My daughter was looking at me and smiling.

This huge wave of realization that my daughter was gone crashed into me again. For the first time, I felt that I had to let her go. Every single cell of my body could feel that scary reality that she had left us. She had left and had taken her promising future with her, leaving us as if dangling from a cliff.

I screamed as loud as I could, "Alina, where did you go? Oh my God, Alina, where are you?" I screamed from the top of my lungs and hit the front panel so hard. I cried and screamed as never before. I did not even feel human. I felt like I was some enraged wild animal. If I had to let her go, I desperately needed to know where she had gone. I kept screaming wildly, "Where are you, Alina? Where are you?"

We headed to the cemetery. We took two chairs, planning to stay with our daughter for a while, and then we were going to visit Yan's grandmother, the sweetest woman, who was under hospice care and was nearly 90 years old. She could not take the fact that her 20-year-old great-granddaughter was gone yet she was still alive. Her body started shutting down shortly after she had seen her great-granddaughter in a casket. She told us that she saw Alina in her dreams almost every night. Alina was wearing her beautiful red dress and running toward her with outstretched arms, trying to hug her.

When our son's daughter had been born a few months before Yan's grandma had turned 90, I thought we should take a nice birthday photo of all the girls of different generations. Five generations from a 90-year-old grandma to a few-months-old baby. Our family chain was broken now.

We put the chairs next to Alina's grave and sat down. Right after, Yan said, "OK, my sweetheart, your room is empty now. You're free to fly, my beautiful angel," his phone rang. He hung up in a few seconds after answering it. He looked at me with his eyes filled with tears and agony. "That's it... Grandma just died."

I started crying. "Oh my God! I just let my daughter go, and she took her favorite babushka with her!"

We folded our chairs and drove straight to Yan's grandma's house. She lived in one of those high-rise senior citizen buildings. I walked into her bedroom. Her breathless body looked very peaceful. "Oh my God, she is with Alina now! I wish it were me instead!"

Yan and I waited in the hallway while the coroners prepared to take our grandma away. My mind went crazy again; I felt like I went back to October 8th, and it was my daughter whom the coroners were taking away. The numbness and fog wore off as the reality sank in deeper and deeper. The pain was unbearable. The realization that my daughter was never coming back ripped my heart into a million pieces. I cried. Loudly. Very loudly. Making the neighbors stick their heads out of their doors to ask if I was ok. I was not ok at all.

Then, I stood at the end of the hallway, watching the gurney with our grandma's covered body move farther and farther away. My mind and my body were experiencing all those feelings I had become numb to on October 8th. The scene that morning was still very fresh in my mind. I had felt so much pain picturing how the lifeless body of my poor child had been taken away by the coroners that day. I was feeling everything now. The pain rippled from my heart in shockwaves through my entire being. I could hardly stand it physically. As I said "goodbye" to our grandma, I was accepting that I was also saying "goodbye" to my child.

Chapter 10: Investigation

Alina's pictures and her story were all over the news. Her beautiful face smiling at me from our big screen TV was followed by the ugly face of the monster who had destroyed such a beauty and the tools that he had used to commit his evil act: a claw hammer and two knives.

I was so thankful to God to learn that my daughter had not suffered. The investigation examiner confirmed that Alina had died immediately from a severe head trauma. The fact that she was gone in a second without suffering brought us some peace.

With no knowledge about what the investigation process was supposed to be, I had assumed that it would be quick. I thought that under the present circumstances, Darby would be sentenced in no time and immediately sent to prison. To my shock, our detectives informed us that we would likely be stuck in their company for the next two to three years as the process unfolded.

Day by day, we became more familiar with the events and procedures related to such an unknown world. The world of violence and crime. We had endless meetings with the detectives, prosecutors, and service people from a center for victims of a crime.

I could not believe what a turn our life had taken. After having been a part of the beautiful world of performing arts that our daughter had a passion for and had introduced us to, we had stepped into this dark world.

Our daughter was brilliantly talented. Alina was a naturally gifted actress, singer, and dancer. Through her talent, she had always brought tears and smiles to the audience, earning so much applause.

I could not believe that after having been in the audience, spending many years of joy watching our beautiful daughter perform on so many stages all over town, we had become the actors on stage ourselves. I could not believe we had taken the roles of victims on the stage of crime.

We knew that we would not be able to handle being on that stage without the help of an attorney. Robert Del Greco, a well-known attorney, had been recommended to us, and he was honored to represent our family in such an extraordinary case. Bobby, his partner Albert, and their assistant Ember became our good friends and guided us with a flashlight through the dark tunnel of that scary process.

Darby was arrested on the day of Alina's funeral, and a preliminary hearing was scheduled a short time after. The anxiety and anticipation were overwhelming. We were going to face the person who had murdered our daughter. I would play that scene in my head over and over again. I was not sure if I would be able to handle it.

Early that morning, Yan, Artem, Kate, and I arrived at the courthouse. I was shaking, not knowing what to expect. We took our seats in the front row and waited. Waited for the monster to walk in. No one from our family had ever seen him or knew anything about him. Alina had never shared anything with us about her relationship with him or the fact that she was being abused by him.

We sat and waited for the moment we would have to face the monster. We had our lawyers by our side and a big support group of friends waiting with us.

And then the door opened. The monster appeared. Without blinking, I watched him walk through the door and approach his spot in front of the judge. I wanted to scream. We were not allowed to say a word. Yan sarcastically made a short comment, "Hi there," and one of our detectives immediately took his chair and placed it next to Yan to make sure Yan would stay under control. Artem sat next to me on the other side. He nervously started tapping his foot. I could feel he was fighting his own monster from jumping out of his body. His wife was gently petting his leg, trying to calm him down.

We all were in shock, wondering how our beautiful girl could be attracted to him. Our prosecutor made the introduction and read the list of injuries that had been done to Alina's body. She went on and on, naming every entry on that list. I felt like I was about to faint as I listened to all the details; it sounded like that list would never end. I had noted some of those atrocities at the scene, but I could not even imagine that so many more had been done in addition to what I had seen with my own eyes. People in the room cried as the prosecutor revealed such unimaginable details.

I could not take my eyes off of that monster. I imagined what thoughts were running through his mind and what he was feeling as he was presented to the audience in this way. He looked very cold and arrogant. His megalomania made me sick to my stomach.

He stood just a few feet away behind the bar. My son told me later that he was having a hard time fighting his urge to jump over that bar and punch him as hard as he could.

Yan was fighting his anger too. What could a loving father feel toward a monster that had brutally and intentionally destroyed his beautiful baby other than the urge to brutally and intentionally destroy that monster? We all had a hard time controlling our emotions.

He stood facing the judge, his back to us, but I could see his side view. I stared at his hands, picturing how those hands made such evil. He did not express any feelings other than his satisfaction.

I was disgusted. I wanted to scream into his disgusting face about how he could do that to my child. Then I watched him pick up his eyeglasses from the table, slowly put them on, and turn to see the crowd behind him. His curious look locked onto me.

I felt as if I had just been shocked by a taser. I could not help my urge to say something to him. Sarcastically, I muttered, "Oh, hey, hello," and then I called him a name in Russian so no one could understand. He immediately got a warning that he should face the judge only.

There was more than enough evidence to go to trial, and we had been warned that the trial would be a long and painful. But we were ready to go through it to the very end. That evil deserved to be washed out from the earth. Our prosecutor was going for the death penalty, and that decision was supported by every single person I knew. It felt that the whole world wanted him to die and burn in hell for eternity.

Chapter 11: Tattoo

Growing up in Russia, embracing Russian culture and traditions, I've inherited a very negative reaction toward piercings and tattoos. A single earring in each ear was the only appropriate thing that I could accept as an accessory to amplify the natural beauty of the human body. Any other piercings or ink was considered disrespectful and humiliating to a family. Alina always called us the old generation and had her own views on life, though. She always had so much respect for her family but also had a strong feeling of belonging to a new generation that liked pushing boundaries.

I always try to understand my kids and look at the world through their eyes whenever they faced obstacles and needed advice and support in making a decision. I also try to understand and respect their choices. Yan has always been a strict father who wanted his kids to only make smart choices in life. In the kids' eyes, he was both a very loving and supportive daddy who always joked around but, at the same time, a very serious father and a life teacher who knew what was right and wrong.

Alina wanted to get a tattoo, but that was absolutely prohibited. She would always tease me, saying that she could not wait to turn eighteen so she would no longer need a parent's permission. She knew exactly what tattoo she wanted to get and tried to convince us to approve of her decision. She really wanted to get a word such as "gratitude" in Russian inked on the side of her body. I could not believe she was going to do that and would flip out every time she tried to make peace on this topic. This was *not* a case where I tried to understand or support her generation's view on life.

She would say, "Mom, how can you not understand how much it means to me? I am so grateful for what you and Dad have done for me, and it's very important for me to express my gratitude to my parents. I am doing it out of appreciation for my parents. Please understand that I'm doing it for you."

My understanding was completely opposite from hers. I really thought that getting a tattoo was such a stupid decision, and I was upset. I warned her that she might regret it later. She wouldn't listen and with a smile on her face always said, "No, Mom, I will never regret it. Just accept it. I will get it done anyway. You just don't understand, but it's ok, Mom, one day you will." But I knew that nothing ever could make me understand such a stupid decision. "No, no, no, I will never understand that, Alina."

One day I got a text message from Alina informing me that she had scheduled her tattoo appointment. At the time, she lived in her dorm on the Greensburg campus. I freaked out and tried everything I could to change her mind, but she was determined.

I was so disappointed and heartbroken. Yan was irate. We didn't talk to her for two weeks. I had never felt so much disappointment in my daughter. The whole family was upset by her choice. She was judged by everyone in the family, and we were embarrassed.

As time went on, we all got over it. That tattoo was hidden under her clothes, so I never worried about it. I knew it would not get exposed to the crowd when she would be wearing her doctor of physical therapy gown one day. I knew she was still smart and beautiful.

Just a couple months before Alina was gone, I found out that she had gotten another tattoo. A little crown on her chest representing strength, power, independence, and freedom. Two months after her disappearance from this earth, I got a strong feeling about getting a tattoo for myself. I could not explain that urge, but I really felt that it would help me feel closer to my daughter and connect me with her somehow.

I wanted to get the same crown that she had. But I didn't want this crown to be hidden from people's eyes. I wanted it to be big. I wanted that crown to scream from my arm telling people how proud I was of my daughter. I was afraid of Yan's reaction though. I thought he might feel negative about it. But he didn't. He cried when I told him. I didn't have to explain anything. He could feel me; it meant so much to him too.

I found the man who had tattooed Alina's crown, and he was more than glad to work on my tattoo. He remembered Alina very well. He created a beautiful work of art on the inside of my left arm: an empress crown with a purple heart inside. The purple heart represents domestic violence awareness, and it means so much to me. My daughter's name is written right under the crown. Alina!

My beautiful child! My power, my strength, my inspiration! I had always had a special connection with my daughter, and that crown tattoo had transformed that connection on a different level. Our connection became more profound, deeper. "Mom, you will understand one day," played in my head over and over again. I felt and understood my daughter's words very well now. They were much more than just words.

I just loved my tattoo so much. Very often I would walk around the house holding my left arm as if it were a baby. My little baby girl, my child, was always with me now.

I was very excited, so I called my mom to reveal the news about my tattoo, expecting her to understand my feelings. But she didn't. She cried, saying, "Oh my God, why would you do that? That ink is going to stay on you forever." I tried to explain to her that it was not just ink; it meant so much to me, and I *wanted* it to stay with me forever. She did not get it. She told my whole family in Russia that I had lost my mind.

I was so heartbroken. I cried so much. I wanted her to understand, but she did not. The same way I could not understand my daughter back then was the same way my mom couldn't understand me now. I felt so hurt from the guilt of not being able to understand my daughter when she had needed to be understood.

Yan loved my tattoo very much and thought about getting one for himself too. He wanted to get a portrait of his beautiful daughter on his left arm. I found a very good tattoo salon, and the owner felt honored to create such meaningful artwork for Yan.

One day, my daughter's big brown eyes were looking at me from my husband's left arm. They were not screaming, "How come, Mom?" anymore. They were saying, "It's ok, Mom." The same portrait of our beautiful daughter in the living room is now forever inked on Yan's left arm. The artwork is beautiful. Daddy's beautiful girl has become a part of my husband's body. "Forever in my heart" is beautifully written underneath. Every night in bed, I stare into my child's eyes that look back at me from my husband's left arm, and I say, "Good night, my sweetheart, I do understand."

Chapter 12: Monument

Alina's grave looked very distinguished. There was a high flower stand with a purple plate attached. ALINA SHEYKHET 07/07/1997 – 10/08/2017 with her beautiful picture underneath. Artem had a hard time looking at those dates sitting next to each other. The date when his sister was born was followed by the date of his own birthday.

A couple of days after Alina's funeral, we took Benji with us to visit her grave. He had been missing his mommy so much. We parked a hundred feet away from Alina's grave. There was a long concrete path to walk. Benji got out of the car and ran all the way to the end of that path, then made a turn and headed toward Alina. We rushed to follow him and could not believe that he ran in the right direction as if he already knew exactly where to go. He ran toward Alina's area and sat at her grave, waiting for us. He knew Alina was there.

That spot in the cemetery always has flowers. We constantly change the decorations for each holiday. I want my daughter to enjoy the holidays no matter where she is. Her new room looked as pretty and cozy as all of her other rooms had always been. Yan was at the cemetery almost every day and had become friends with all the groundskeepers. Everybody felt for him, watching how he took care of his daughter's grave and offering their help.

None of the cemetery cleaning affected Alina's area. None of her flowers and decorations have ever been touched by the cleaning people.

It was time to work on Alina's headstone. The *monument* for my *daughter*. These two words don't belong in the same sentence. Yan wanted to go to the same place where he had worked on his father's monument just a few months ago. Yan liked working with that company, and they had done a beautiful job making his dad's headstone. Alina had gone there with Yan a few times. She had helped Yan make a design, so they knew her there. Those people had a hard time believing that Alina needed a monument for herself this time.

It took me forever to agree on the final design. For a few months we went back and forth with a designer. I just wanted her monument to be as pretty as she was. That was very hard to accomplish. I'm not sure if my brain fully comprehended what I was doing. I still am not able to comprehend it. I don't think any parent ever would be able to. Making a design for your child's headstone could never sound real for any parent on earth.

It was so hard to explain what changes I wanted to make over the phone. So every time, Yan and I drove to their office, and I tried to draw my ideas. And every time we left their office, I was completely destroyed. I thought I would never agree to send that project to production. I never felt satisfied. In reality, I didn't want this project to exist at all.

But I understood it needed to be finished. Another unimaginable challenge needed to be overcome. I tried my best to stay strong and control the emotions overwhelming me during our visits to the monument company. One day, we received the final sketch. I could not stop crying looking at it. It was absolutely gorgeous.

A shiny black, five-foot-tall curved stone had the big, beautiful eyes of my daughter at the top. Her eyes mesmerized me. They were looking so deep inside of me, telling me, "Mom, I am very grateful for everything you and Dad have done for me." The full body of my child was engraved underneath those eyes. My beautiful daughter was leaning on a swing. She was smiling at me almost saying, "I love you, Mom," with her body language. Benji's paw was printed at the edge of the swing, and on the side, a bouquet of her favorite flowers, Russian daisies, complemented her beautiful dress. **Alina Sheykhet, Forever in our hearts**. On the back was a big crown with a purple heart inside, her name engraved in Russian, and a ballerina surrounded by the words that had been written on the wall in Alina's bedroom, "**Sing Dance Love.**" I could not stop crying. The sketch was approved and sent to production.

The stone was ready to be set up at the time when Alina's friends were graduating college. The happy faces of her friends in their caps and gowns were all over Facebook. My heart was breaking for my daughter. I remembered how determined she had been to become a doctor. I looked at the pictures of all the proud parents and thought about how one day Alina had randomly said, "Guys! Look at me! The future doctor of physical therapy is right in front of you! Dr. Alina Sheykhet, PhD. I promise you, right here and right now, that very soon you will be so proud of your daughter." I remembered how proud we already were at that moment and how much we laughed, reminding her that she had to finish high school first.

While other parents were enjoying the graduation ceremonies of their kids, Yan and I were getting ready to see the headstone of our "future doctor." I was very anxious. I was so afraid to see it. It felt like validation that she was really gone. Often, when I sat at the kitchen island and stared at the empty bar stool where Alina always sat, I thought it all had to be a cruel joke and that she would just come in and laugh, "Hey, guys, that's it, I was just kidding . . . it's over." Seeing that headstone meant that it was not a joke. It was for real. I didn't want to see that damn stone at all.

Yan drove through the cemetery to Alina's grave. From far away, Yan could see that the stone was up. "Oh my God, it's there," he said shakily. My whole body trembled. "It's covered. I asked them to cover it."

He nervously parked, and we rushed to the grave. We stared silently at the covered monument and didn't know what to do next. I took a picture of it and sent it to my son. He got emotional. I sent the picture to my mother-in-law, and she wanted to come to the cemetery immediately to see her granddaughter and share this devastating moment with us. Right in that moment, one of our friends called, and Yan asked him to bring his mom. We nervously waited for them to come.

Time moved slowly. I could not wait any longer. I panicked, running around the stone, feeling like I was looking at Alina's closed casket again. I finally yelled, "Yan, just open it . . . I can't anymore."

I nervously watched my husband's shaking hands slowly remove the wrapping from our child's headstone. His beautiful daughter, his future doctor of physical therapy, smiled at him from her monument. He burst into tears. I froze. I could not believe what I was seeing. The *Monument* for my *Daughter*. I played these two foreign words in my head as one phrase now. These two words danced in my mind as if they were one inseparable couple, forever engaged. Beauty and the Beast. Even though I felt horrible, I was not disappointed by what appeared in front of me. Through the lens of heavy tears in my devastated eyes, I looked at one perfectly made piece of art. The monument was beautiful. It looked perfect. My daughter's big beautiful eyes stared at me and sadly said, "I'm sorry, Mom, I didn't keep my promise." And then, tears slowly rolled down my face. I didn't need these apologies. I always felt very proud of her. I knew she was still beautiful and smart no matter where she was. I knew she was grateful for everything we had done for her.

Chapter 13: Grief

I have experienced a few losses in my life. Some of my friends in Russia died young, and I had been shocked to learn about their passing. I had buried all of my grandparents. I had to say "goodbye" to Yan's father. We had a special bond with him, and I called him "Dad." All these losses were heartbreaking, especially the loss of my father-in-law, but none of them could be compared to the loss of my daughter. The emotions associated with that event were so unknown and unbearable to me. To move on and just keep going was not an option. Parents can never let go of their child and move on. It's just impossible. Instead, they need to learn how to move forward as they carry that loss.

The weight of that loss was heavy, like an unmovable boulder. It took a lot of effort to keep walking and carrying that boulder. It could not be dropped even for a moment. The edges of it were sharp, and with every step I took, it cut me. The more I moved, the more I bled. It was painful and exhausting.

The thought that I would never see my daughter again pushed me into an ugly, scary place. Comprehending the definition of "never" caused a horrible panic attack. Every day, sitting in my office, I stared at Alina's picture, trying to understand where she was. I could not find an answer. Looking at my daughter and realizing that she was associated with "never" and "nowhere" shook me to the core. The panic attacks hit me hard. I had never experienced a panic attack before, so I had no idea how scary they could feel. I was so scared to feel scared because I didn't know how to deal with that feeling. Every time a wave of panic hit, I left my office and ran around the floor, trying to get some air. My chest would get heavy, and it was hard to breathe. I became scared of my existence. The fear of living without my daughter was overwhelming, and I just wanted to escape this world.

I desperately wanted to fix my life but knew it could never be fixed, which gave me so much anxiety. I felt as though I had been picked up and dangled over a cliff, threatened with being dropped. Whenever I had faced difficulties before, I was always able to calm myself with the positive thought that it was only temporary and that I just needed to wait until everything went back to normal. But my daughter's death was not temporary. That issue was permanent. I could not reach my normal positive thoughts because I realized that I could not wait patiently for the difficult days to pass, for the sun to change the clouds and for my daughter to reappear. No matter what I did or however long I waited, nothing would ever change. My daughter was going to be dead forever. Such a negative, permanent outcome led me to be trapped in a maze of fear. From a psychological perspective, I didn't see how my mind could ever calm down and feel peace again.

That wave of panic was followed by a wave of anger and disappointment. I was angry at the people around me because they still had their normal lives. They had normal conversations about kids, holidays, vacations, even a simple chat about nothing. People around me had stayed the same. Nothing had changed for them. But my whole being had changed forever, and I wanted people to acknowledge that. I could not look the same, I could not think the same, and I could not have those normal conversations about life anymore. I desperately needed people to change with me too. But I knew that was not how the world worked.

It was so tiring to try to fit into that world now. I had to wear an "I am ok" mask around other people; I had to put on a fake smile and participate in their normal conversations about their normal lives; I had to fake my normalcy. It stirred feelings of disappointment. I hurt because people could not understand me or what I was feeling. They were incapable of understanding because their children were alive. My feelings could not be described or explained or compared to anything else. I belonged to a different world now: the world of bereaved parents. The world that was unknown to all others around me.

That wave of anger was replaced by a wave of sadness and depression. I could not stop crying. I felt pity for my daughter because she had been a victim. I thought she must be so mad for having been removed from us. I felt as if she was miserable and tortured. It felt very unfair that I was still here yet she was not allowed to be with us anymore. Yet, people around me were feeling pity for ME.

Hearing "Oh, my heart breaks for you... I can't imagine what you're going through" was so hurtful. It was not about me at all. I didn't care how hurt I was. It was all about my child! My heart was breaking for HER because I could imagine very well what she was going through as a "non-alive human being." I had always been terrified of becoming a non-alive human being one day, and my daughter was one already. She was at that place that I had always been afraid of. It petrified me. It was not about me because no matter what, I was still alive, but my daughter was not. And people just did not get it. I wanted to be alone. It was easier to deal with my new world and all my feelings and emotions when I was alone.

I became distant from everything and everyone. I pushed away my friends, and I had no desire to talk to my relatives. I could not even talk to my mom. The emotions were insane. It felt like everyone was saying the wrong words and giving me advice that I didn't need. My friends and family wanted me to feel better, but I didn't see how a mother could ever feel good if her child was forever dead.

I was not able to attend any parties or celebrations for my friends. I felt like I was a prisoner in a concentration camp, and it was impossible to explain to them how I felt. I thought it was unnatural and inappropriate to enjoy celebrations or even gatherings. Everything hurt physically and emotionally. I was a prisoner, forever suffering.

It was very hard to spend time with my son and his family as well. It was so hard to feel happy for them. Every happy event in their lives felt like a hard punch to my face, reminding me that Alina could not have it or could not do it. I wanted to feel happy for my son, for my daughter-in-law, and for my granddaughter, but my heart was bleeding, bleeding hard. Feeling love for them felt like I was betraying Alina. Family functions were excruciating. Alina's chair was always empty. And during every single second of every minute of each day, I felt the presence of her absence. The happiness of my son and his wife hurt me, but it was impossible to explain, so I tried to smile and express happiness as my heart silently screamed in pain. My heart wanted Alina to be happy too.

Often my heart felt as if she had been kidnapped and tortured and was crying for help, and the only person who could understand my feelings was my husband. I didn't need to give him any explanation; he felt exactly what I felt.

Isolation brought me some comfort because I didn't have to try to seem normal. After eight hours of being among people at work and faking normalcy, I needed to be in my shell for the rest of the day. The weekends were the worst. I didn't want to see anyone and didn't want to be engaged in other people's conversations. Witnessing the world keep going without Alina was extremely painful.

The waves of grief came and went, giving me a little time to breathe between them. I knew they would never stop coming, and I was painfully learning how to survive them. I was learning how to surf them. If you tried to fight those waves, they would knock you down, and you'd sink into an ocean of never-ending suffering. So I had to learn how to stop fighting them and become "friends" instead. I had to learn how to cooperate with each coming wave so it would make its ugly dance under my feet more smoothly. I had to accept all the scratches, the hits, the stabs, the wounds. I had to learn how to endure that unbearable pain in peace.

Chapter 14: Bereaved Parents Club

The moment Alina was gone, Yan and I became members of a club that no one ever thinks they'll join. The club that doesn't get its members voluntarily. Every single member of that club gets thrown into it without being asked. Not in a million years would Yan and I have thought we would become members one day.

The bereaved parents club. Once you join, you can't quit it or escape from it. You automatically become a lifetime member. The price of your membership is very high. It costs you the life of your child.

I didn't even know such a club existed. I always believed that kids just don't die. For forty-five years, I had lived in a bubble, surrounded by normal families whose children had always been alive. I knew some accidents and tragedies had taken place in the world. But those events were so far away and felt like a movie. My daughter's death was not a movie, and it was very hard to face as a reality. It had no logic. What had been done to my child and my family was beyond my comprehension. I kept asking myself how it could have happened to my daughter if it just does not happen. THIS never happens. I went looking for answers.

I discovered many Facebook groups where bereaved parents shared their stories. Most people in those groups were moms. I rarely saw the dads join. The discussion topics could not be shared on their normal Facebook pages. These discussions were like a secret that bereaved moms were not comfortable sharing with the rest of the world. The group was a safe place where these moms could share their grief without being judged or misunderstood because all those moms walked in the same shoes, the shoes of a mother who had lost her child. I got a pair of those ugly shoes too. I became one of those moms.

Every night I read their posts. I never shared anything about myself and never made any comments. I just scrolled down, reading non-stop stories from heartbroken mothers. It was very shocking to learn how many bereaved parents were out there. Their children were all ages from newborns to young adults. Children who had died of different causes—cancer, overdose, suicide, murder, car crash, hit by a car, drowning, falling, fire, cardiac arrest, asthma attack, a myriad of unimaginable tragic accidents, and many more. I had no idea that so many families were suffering. My family had always been happy, and so had all the other families around me. I had no idea these heartbroken parents had always been walking in a crowd right next to me, pretending to be normal.

I looked at the faces of those children with the amazement of how beautiful every single face was. It seemed like those kids were special; they were chosen. Their personalities were described as happy, loving, caring, and full of life.

Every day I scrolled down and stared at those faces. New ones kept popping up. Children kept dying and leaving their parents forever broken. After seeing hundreds of faces and reading hundreds of unbelievable stories, I realized that it did happen. My daughter was not the only one, and I was just one of so many broken mothers. This whole new world had been opened wide, and it was "welcoming" me.

The population of my new world was very big. It seemed like it was as large as my old world was. And that was shocking to me. I realized that there had always been two worlds: the normal one of families with living kids and the abnormal one, the scary world of families whose children were dead. I learned that the normal world was not aware of how scary the other world was. Also, I learned that no parents were guaranteed to stay in that normal world forever. Today you belonged to your normal beautiful world, but tomorrow you could be thrown into such an ugly place you never knew existed.

The biggest challenge was that every day you had to witness the happy and beautiful functioning of your old world while trying to accept the fact that you didn't belong there anymore. Everyday people of your old world would try to engage you in their daily activities. Holidays, parties, birthdays, graduations, weddings, and other things that used to be your reality too. They saw you as still existing in their world, assuming that you were still a part of it. But you were not. What they saw was only a shadow of you. Because you lived in a different reality. From time to time, you would let your shadow be engaged in those activities with others. But the real YOU was never there. The real YOU was quietly sitting in your new world and painfully watching how your shadow was trying to fit in to the place where you used to belong.

I realized that instead of dwelling on my old world where I was just a shadow, I needed to become active here and explore my new place. I needed to see what people of this world looked like, what they said, and how they acted. I had so many questions and hoped to find some answers by interacting with my new community.

I learned about The Compassionate Friends USA. It was a national nonprofit offering help and hope to families grieving the death of a child. I contacted one of their presenters, Mitch Carmody. He was a writer, artist, grief educator, and nationally recognized speaker. Mitch had experienced the loss of his son followed by grieving and was giving his messages of hope to other parents. He responded with a compassionate message and gave me his advice on certain things related to grieving. Also, he invited Yan and me to one of his upcoming events.

It was going to be a Day of Hope event, organized by The Healing Heart Foundation, and it would be dedicated to the victims of the Parkland School shooting that had happened just a couple months ago. Yan and I had been very affected by that tragedy, and we wanted to attend the event and meet the parents of those children who had been shot on that horrific day, the parents who had become new members of our club. The bereaved parents club was growing each day.

Chapter 15: Trip to Florida

Yan and I planned a trip to Florida to attend the Day of Hope event. That was going to be our first trip without Alina. I did not know what to expect because we used to travel a lot, and Alina had always been with us. I knew it was going to be very hard, but I was ready to face that challenge.

Packing was tough. Alina's pile of clothes was missing, and I could not stop crying. I felt so much guilt going on a trip without her, as if I was betraying her. When Yan and I had planned our last trip to Russia, we jokingly said she was better off staying home and studying. She got so mad at our joke and frowned at us like a little girl.

"How could you do it to your own child?" she said. "No, you will never go anywhere without me. Don't even try. I would be mad for the rest of my life and would never forgive you." She was so cute when she got mad, and we always laughed at her.

The whole time we were on the airplane, I heard Alina's voice, "Mom, I wish I was going with you." I was not doing well at all; the feeling of guilt was eating me inside. My mind had to work hard to shift its "I'm going on vacation" mode, triggered by being on the plane, to a different perception. I convinced my mind to perceive it as a necessary self-survival act. I cried the whole time we were in the air.

We landed at the Miami airport. I could not stop thinking about Alina walking to this same gate just two months before she had died. She was visiting her friend in Miami, and it was her last trip. I pictured her pulling her super cute leopard print suitcase that we had gotten her for that trip. I could clearly hear the clicking of that suitcase's wheels and Alina's infectious laugh. I could not stop crying.

Just a few minutes away from the airport is a park we knew Alina had visited during her trip. The place was called Wynwood Walls, a destination featuring huge, colorful street murals by artists from around the globe. Alina had taken so many pictures by the walls, and one of them had been chosen for a t-shirt design that her friends had made in her memory. So we wanted to visit The Walls.

Walking there was not easy either. The place was beautiful. Very colorful. I could see my daughter crazily running from one wall to another, trying to take a picture of every single painting. We could not find the one that had been used for Alina's t-shirt design. It seemed odd that one girl, a victim of the Parkland shooting, had had her picture taken at that wall too. I remembered looking at the pictures of those students after the shooting had happened, and I got chills when I saw a picture of a tiny, beautiful girl standing by the same wall that Alina had stood by.

That painting was not there. It seemed like the murals from that time had been replaced with new ones. I got chills all over my body. It meant that both Alina and that poor Parkland girl had been there at the same time just shortly before their lives had been taken away.

That night at the hotel was such a nightmare. My anxiety was high. I was trying to fall asleep, but every time I did, Alina's voice would wake me up. "Mom." I was nervous about the next morning, te morning when we would meet other members of our club for the first time.

Yan and I were sitting in the hotel restaurant, waiting for our breakfast to be served. I felt weird. The event was going to take place in our hotel's conference room shortly, and I wondered if these people at the restaurant were the parents whom I was so anxious to meet. Everybody looked normal to me. I felt like the only abnormal one there, and Alina's voice kept screaming in my head, "Mom."

I heard the ding of a text message. I looked at my phone and almost dropped it from what I saw. It was a message from my son. Artem had never been a sweet-talker in his texts. Being a typical guy, he would just say a simple "hi" followed by a short message.

This time his message was "Mom," something his sister would usually do. She would randomly text me "Mom" and wait for my response, "Yes, dochka," before she would tell me a story from her life. My son never did that. He sounded like Alina this morning. Again, it made me cry.

The conference was about to start. We entered the conference room, where two ladies greeted us by the check-in table. They asked if we were presenters or bereaved parents. I had a hard time opening my mouth to say who we were. They asked us to register and put on a tag with Alina's name. I felt very weird and very hurt. I did not like this at all.

There were so many people around. Everyone looked surprisingly normal. Other people were talking and smiling. But I didn't feel like talking or smiling. We kept looking around, and then I saw a familiar face. It was Mitch Carmody. Yan said I should go talk to him and let him know we were there. I hesitated. I felt shy and uncomfortable.

Mitch was so glad to see us. He gave us a hug and explained what would be going on at the conference. A few presenters would give their speeches, and afterward, there would be different workshops and meetings with counselors.

Yan and I entered the auditorium where the welcome part was supposed to happen. We quietly took our seats and started observing again. The stage was being prepared for the speakers, and there was a camera guy there. One by one, people introduced themselves to the camera, saying whom they had lost and delivering their messages. We didn't join in. There was a huge poster on the wall. Pictures of all these kids who had lost their lives in the shooting that had taken place just a few miles away. I kept staring at them. Once again, all those faces were beautiful and looked very special. I shifted my eyes from one to another, asking the same question, "Where did you go?" I desperately needed to know where all these beautiful children had gone. Because they were now in the same place my daughter was. The feeling of unknowingness was terrifying, but knowing that my daughter was with those children now calmed me, to some degree.

The president of the Healing Heart Foundation went on stage and revealed his story about how he had lost his daughter, how this organization was established, and how they were helping parents who had lost their children. Other presenters delivered their messages of hope to the parents. I looked around, trying to figure out which ones were the parents of the kids whose pictures were on the wall. I felt emotional.

One of the survivors, a student of the school where the shooting had taken place, went on stage. He had written a song and dedicated it to his friends who had not survived that horrific day. It was a rap song. I had chills all over my body listening to him sing. His message was deeply touching. The audience was silent. It seemed no one was even breathing. Tears were silently running down people's sad faces, and seventeen happy faces on the wall were looking down at the heartbroken audience and smiling.

The atmosphere was intense. Suddenly the silence was interrupted by a loud sound as one side of that huge poster detached from the wall and loudly dropped down. I jumped in my chair.. "Oh my God," I said to Yan. "They are here." I really felt like those kids had intentionally detached the poster to get the attention of the audience, their parents.

After we left the welcome presentation, we attended a parents meeting with counselors from New York City. There were about twenty people in our group. We all gathered in a circle. Two ladies, the professional grief counselors, introduced themselves and asked us to introduce ourselves. The families were from different states, and they told their stories of what had happened to their children. None of the parents in that room had children die at Parkland. There was one family with three children who were survivors of that shooting. The mom said how terrified they had been that day and how traumatized their children had become. She said her kids were experiencing the trauma of survivor's guilt and were seeking help. I didn't even know such a trauma existed. Instead of being thankful for surviving, the students felt so much guilt instead. They had a hard time coping with life after witnessing their friends die. (And as I learned later, one of the survivors took her own life a year after the tragedy.)

When it was my turn to introduce myself, it was the first time I introduced myself as a mother who had lost her child. For the first time, I opened my mouth and said out loud that Alina had been murdered. It had been six months since Alina was gone, and my mouth had not been able to form the word "murdered" after saying her name. But I said it here for the first time. Yan cried. With my voice shaking, I briefly told Alina's story to the group. I could not hold back my tears.

The counselors shared their experiences working with people after experiencing a tragedy. One of them had worked with families affected by the 9/11 attack, and she said that she was still working with some of them. It had been seventeen years, but people still needed help because their trauma was very deep. She warned us about PTSD, which usually happened after a tragic loss, and gave us some advice on what to do to possibly prevent that. Also, she said that after a tragic loss, it might take a year before you could work with a counselor. She explained that your system goes into shock and runs in survival mode by creating a blockage and numbness in response to such great trauma.

In the first year, your system is not ready for healing. After severe damage to your physical body, it takes time for your wounds to heal before you can start doing physical therapy, and it's the same way after severe emotional trauma — your mental wounds must also heal before you can start mental therapy. All you can do for the first year is be gentle with yourself and slowly let the grief run through your body, accepting all the pain and emotions. To me, it sounded like I should be in the intensive care unit limiting the movement of my body. But instead, I was trying to move forward, constantly reopening the wounds. I immediately remembered the words of our counselor Wendy. "Be gentle with yourself and let the pain and grief run through your body."

I felt overwhelmed and completely destroyed. After a lunch break, we decided not to return but to go to the beach instead. That did not go well either. I cried the whole time. I didn't want to "enjoy" the beach; I didn't want to do anything without my daughter. The pain was so intense; it was so hard to endure it. We got back to the hotel and stayed there for the rest of the day. I hated everything and didn't want to be there. I wanted to be where Alina was. I didn't know what that place was, and I was very afraid of it, but if she was there and so were these beautiful Parkland kids, I wanted to be with them no matter where they were.

Late in the evening, we went to dinner at our hotel restaurant. It was crowded and loud. People were enjoying each other's company; they all looked happy. I could not stand their loud laughing. It was so painful to stay in that environment. "Oh my God, look who is here," Yan said. All the presenters from the morning event were there too. All these people who had talked about the shooting tragedy, about their loss and grief, sat at a table, enjoying their dinner and smiling and laughing like everyone else was. That made me feel sick to my stomach. All of them had lost their children — how could they dare enjoy themselves and laugh. I looked at the people of my new world and thought that I would never belong with them. I would never want to enjoy my life and laugh again. To me, it felt as if they didn't care that their children were dead. That was unacceptable to me.

The next day, we returned home. I was completely lost. I didn't think I could survive another day. I desperately needed to know where my daughter was. I knew she could not just disappear and go nowhere. She had to be somewhere, and there had to be a reason why she went there. There had to be a reason for all those beautiful children leaving this world, and I had to find out.

Chapter 16: Looking for Answers

After what happened to Alina and after learning about all those other young children who had left their parents, I sought the answer to one question. Why? Why did some people get to live till their 90s, yet other people had been given such a short time on this earth? I knew that no one could stay here forever; we were all here only temporarily, so sooner or later, we would all go to the same place. But before knowing where we all would go and where my daughter already was, I had to find out where we all had come from and what for.

I started reading. Along with reading about children dying, I read books to educate myself on a very sensitive topic that most people tried to avoid. I had never been a religious person. I had gone to church just a few times in my life, and those visits had felt very uncomfortable to me. I had never believed in "God." The man described as sitting in a cloud throne, watching people from above to make decisions about whom to punish and whom to praise was just another fairy tale character to me. Believing in such a figure was the same as believing in Santa Claus. I didn't believe in Santa, and I didn't believe in God, but I always felt that I was something more than just "Elly" and wondered who I really was. And when I thought about death, I could not comprehend that there would not be a ME one day.

I did not read religious books. Instead I educated myself in spirituality and became fascinated learning about the spirit world. It felt different from reading the Bible or going to church. It seemed like I was still learning about God but from a different perspective. The information was awe-inspiring and comforted me. The study sources came out of nowhere. It seemed like someone was directing me and telling me where to look and what to read. It felt as though the spirit world were communicating with me.

One day, random info popped up on my Facebook—Dr. Linda Backman, licensed psychologist, regression therapist, and the author of *Bringing your Soul to Light*, was giving an online study course about soul evolution. Without hesitation, I decided to take it.

During this seven-week course, I would discover who I was as a soul, why our souls incarnate, what occurs in between lives, how we "pre-plan" our lives, and what happens when we die. Also, I was going to learn how to tap into my intuition, how to recognize unresolved past lives' circumstances, and how they were meant to enhance my tenacity and evolution.

I successfully finished the course. I learned so much and slowly shifted my understanding about life to a completely different perspective. I knew that I was an eternal spiritual being, and by being in my temporary physical body, I was getting an earthly experience in a present life period. I learned that I had come here to learn lessons and evolve.

I learned that we all sign life agreements before we come to earth. We all choose how long we will stay and what lessons we will learn. We all come in groups, our soul groups. We usually incarnate with the same members of our soul group, but we play different roles in each lifetime. We apply the knowledge and experiences of our past lives to our present life.

More experienced and mature souls might come here just to help less evolved souls grow. Usually these souls don't stay here for a long time. If the lesson has not been learned, we bring the same lesson to our next incarnation and face the same difficulties that we have to overcome and grow from. Sometimes we get stuck with the same problem for a few lives.

Nothing in our life just randomly happens. We plan our life circumstances; we choose our parents and our geographic location. We plan to meet certain people at certain times. In every relationship, either long lasting or very short, we are either teachers or students. We all help each other learn different lessons. And we are all here in the service of love.

The more loving and compassionate we become, the higher level our soul will vibrate at. When we leave our physical body and go back to the spirit world, we go through our lifetime review, and our masters determine how much energy we have gained from being on earth. Depending on how well our soul has been fed with love and compassion by overcoming our life challenges and learning lessons, we move to a different level. With each life we spend on earth, we are supposed to go higher and higher until we get to the level where we do not have to go down to earth to learn anymore. We become teachers and masters and guide other souls toward growth in their experiences on earth. We are energy, and God is the source of our energy. We all are connected and help humanity evolve.

I became fascinated with my study, but I could not share it with others. People around me, people from my old world, had no need to learn about this. They were happy and busy with their earthly things — that's why they had no desire to ask a question like "What happens to me after I die?" Just a few months ago, I had been one of them and had not wanted to bother my mind by thinking about that either. I had just wanted to enjoy the life of my physical body without questions. And had my daughter not left her physical body, I would never have started looking for these answers.

I wanted to scream about what I had discovered. I wanted people to know where my daughter was and where one day we would all go too. But when I tried to share my discovery, people reacted as if I was saying Santa Claus was real. Most people didn't believe in a spirit world, so I tried not to talk about it much because I didn't want to sound as though I had lost my mind.

Yan happened to be the "lucky" one who was forced to listen to "all that crap," as he referred to my study. "You read way too much sh**. You better do something useful instead of sitting on the couch all the time, reading that crap." But I could not stop. I went deeper and deeper into my study. I got answers to all my whys. I had found where my daughter was. I knew why she had left.

My daughter IS a very experienced and mature soul. I have no doubt that she has lived many lives on earth. I had always asked how she could know everything. How could she be so intelligent and mature at her young age? Very often I felt like she was the mother and not me. And I was always amazed by how much she loved people and how easy and natural she was at making connections with different people. She was able to bring something good out of everyone; she could genuinely make people feel special.

As a high-vibrating soul, my daughter had agreed to come here for a short period of time and help other souls grow. She was on a mission. She didn't have to stay long, and she wanted to leave in a way that would make a very profound impact on others. By shaking people to the core, she wanted to help them reevaluate their lives, to change their life perspectives. By sacrificing herself, she wanted to help people awaken and realize who they really were.

I was awakened for sure. They say that grief, hurt, and pain are physical tools that the soul can use as stepping stones to enlightenment.

Chapter 17: Getting Proof

It was still very hard to wrap my head around what I had discovered. Believing and feeling the spirit world was bringing me peace. But it was very hard to stay faithful. It felt like my ego was constantly fighting my soul. It made me doubt my study. It made me doubt my feelings and intuition toward the spirit world. My ego wanted me to think that it was just my imagination. It seemed that feelings of grief and being vulnerable could make me believe even in Santa Claus.

I was dancing between two worlds. The beautiful world of spirits made me feel peaceful by connecting me with my daughter and giving me faith that I would go there one day and be reunited with her. My old world, the world where my physical body belonged, made me feel suffocated because my daughter's physical body was not there.

Just reading about the spirit world and believing in it was not enough. I needed the kind of proof and validation that would create a balance between my two worlds because I kept jumping from one back to another.

I came across the book *Messages of Hope*, written by the psychic-medium Suzanne Giesemann. She is a former U.S. Navy commander who served as a commanding officer and aide to the chairman of the Joint Chiefs of Staff on 9/11. Witnessing the tragedy of 9/11 and the tragic death of her stepdaughter, a sergeant in the Marine Corps who was struck and killed by lightning along with her unborn son, propelled Giesemann in a new direction in search of life's deepest truth and led her to study mediumship. She developed an ability to communicate with those on the other side and provided stunning evidence of life after death. Giesemann is the author of twelve books, and her gift of evidential mediumship has been tested and proven. It seemed that *Message of Hope* was the book I had been looking for as proof of my discovery.

I could not put my new book down. The author told the story of her life and how she had ended up transitioning from being an officer in the Navy to being a medium who could communicate with the spirit world. Her story was breathtaking, and I became a fan. I followed her Facebook and listened to her radio shows. Her guests share their life stories and experiences that were proving that life did indeed exist after we die. I remember how at one show she corrected her guest by saying that the word "die" would be inaccurate in his story because we don't really die—we cross over; we transition into the spirit world. I breathed a sigh of relief after that comment. I believe that Giesemann is a real messenger of hope for people who struggle with the loss of their loved ones.

Bob Olsen, a former skeptic and private investigator, is another author whose book I became attracted to. The painful event of his father's death when Olsen was 35 had led him to investigate the afterlife and research psychic mediums. After 15 years of investigation, he became a leading expert on life after death, psychic mediums, after-death communication, past lives, and near-death experiences. In his book *Answers About The Afterlife*, Olsen answers many of the questions I had. I dove into his work. Olsen is the leading authority on the subject, according to TV, movie, and documentary producers; newspaper journalists; radio hosts; and book publishers. Every night I listened to his radio show and was amazed by the life stories and experiences of his guests and psychic mediums.

Yan was willing to listen to Bob's shows too and had actually become a fan. One night the guest on the show was Robert Schwartz, the author of a book I had read called *Your Soul's Plan*. Schwartz is a spiritual facilitator, international speaker, and practitioner in past life soul regression. Yan and I quietly listened to his explanation that each of us had spirit guides, nonphysical beings with whom we planned our lives prior to incarnation. He revealed the real meaning behind the pre-birth planning of physical illness, having disabled children, deafness, blindness, drug addiction, the death of a loved one, accidents, and other horrible life conditions.

Yan's eyes nearly popped out of his head from such a revelation. He sarcastically said to me, "Are you kidding me? Are you telling me that I had pre-planned everything I am going through now? No freaking way I would've ever planned that. I would have never signed such a damn agreement."

I smiled and replied, "Oh yeah, can you believe that? What the hell were we thinking when we signed that contract?"

That idea became such a therapeutic joke for us. Every time one of us whined or complained about how painful our life had become, the other immediately responded, "You signed that contract, remember? Deal with it now." And very often, when I felt down and cried to Yan about how unfair and tiring our life was, he would give me strength by saying seriously, "It's OK... it's all about getting an experience anyway. I will go through my experience to the end. I won't give up." And often, when Yan was down, I would tell him, "It's OK... we'll do better in the next life."

Dr. Brian Weiss is another specialist whose work I became fascinated with. Dr. Weiss is a psychiatrist, hypnotherapist, and author of many books that specialize in past life regression. In his book *Many Lives, Many Masters*, Dr. Weiss discusses how one of his patients discovered the afterlife. A young woman suffering from anxiety attacks had sought help from him. During sessions of hypnosis, Dr. Weiss brought her memory back to her childhood, trying to find where the issue was rooted. He led her memory further and further back and then realized that it had gone way too far. He actually made her remember a previous life. When she started revealing memories of her past lives, Dr. Weiss said it was such a shocking experience that, as a skeptic, he didn't know how to react.

His skepticism eroded when his patient began to channel messages from "the space between lives" that contained remarkable revelations about Weiss's family and his dead son. Using past life therapy, he was able to cure the patient and embark on a new, more personally meaningful phase of his career.

It seemed I was not even breathing when I read how that woman had told her therapist about who she was and what she was doing in her previous lives. She described how she had died in those lives too. Her anxiety attacks and fears were caused by the traumas from her past lives. That was shocking to me.

Along with reading books giving me the proof I needed about the afterlife, I watched YouTube videos about near-death experiences. People shared about leaving their bodies during clinical death. They would float and watch their bodies from above. All of them experienced an overwhelming feeling of unconditional love and didn't want to go back. They saw the light and were attracted to it. They all said how amazing and life-changing that experience was and how they were not afraid of death anymore because death didn't really exist. One woman, who was very attracted to her physical body and had spent so much money making her body look perfect, described how she felt about that body when she had left it due to a car accident. She said she felt as if she had taken a heavy coat off. It was a very nice coat, and it was well-used, but it felt as if it was time to take it to the Salvation Army. She realized how silly she had been by associating herself with her physical body and paying that much attention to it because you are not your body — you are a soul who uses your body as a vehicle to drive you through life on earth, and it feels amazing when you leave that "heavy car" and fly free without limitation.

Day by day I believed in the afterlife more and more. It brought me peace knowing that Alina was there and she was not alone, but I had a hard time understanding how she could exist without her body. It freaked me out. I knew that one day I would lose my body too, but my human brain could not comprehend how I would function without it.

I had to watch, listen, and read about the place where my daughter was every day. Every morning for me started the same. I woke up at 4 a.m. in a panic attack because my daughter was dead, and just like Drew Barrymore in the movie *50 First Dates*, I did not remember what I had watched, listened, or read about yesterday. Each morning, I woke up to the horror of my child having been brutally murdered, and I was giving up my own life. Then very slowly and patiently, my soul communicated with me and explained what I had watched, listened, and read. My soul helped me remember where my child actually was and why, and I would slowly and painfully shift into my new world and calm down. Some days, it would take me longer to make that shift. Some days I was not able to shift at all, and my unimaginable reality would pull me down to the bottom of a scary place.

Yan had a hard time comprehending all the information that I shared with him, but he really wanted to believe that his daughter had survived and was in a different world waiting for him. One day he confessed that what had helped him the most was the thought that he had chosen this life experience himself and that's why he no longer felt like a victim of the situation. He felt as though he had been tested on his own strength and he was not going to be a failure and give up.

My husband stopped referring to my study as "crap." He had become very supportive and open to that topic. He had let me educate him in spirituality and was always willing to listen to my nonstop stories. A new belief was helping us process our grief and move forward.

Chapter 18: Mediums

I had read so many stories about people's experiences with mediums and wanted to have my own. I desperately wanted to get a reading with a medium and get a message from my daughter. Alina had loved *Long Island Medium*, starring Theresa Caputo, and always asked Yan and me to watch it with her. She would scream from her room, "Guys, oh my God, come here! You have to see this. She is talking to dead people, and she is real." I was never attracted to that show and could not take Caputo as seriously as Alina did. But just because Alina had been fascinated by that medium, I bought tickets to her upcoming show in Erie, Pa., a couple hours north of Pittsburgh.

I had no idea what to expect and was nervous the whole time we were driving to Erie. The theater was packed. There was not one empty seat. Yan and I were still in deep grief and could not handle big crowds, so we were very uncomfortable.

Then, Caputo came on stage. She wore very bright makeup, a very short dress, and super high heels. The audience clapped and cheered. She walked down the aisle, giving messages to randomly selected people. She revealed how their loved ones died, giving evidence from their lives. People were emotional, crying and laughing at the same time. They all validated the information that Caputo was getting from their loved ones.

Though it seemed like she could really communicate with those on the other side, the way she presented such sensitive communication felt inappropriate. She constantly made jokes, swearing from time to time and acting vulgar. I felt like we were at a stand-up comedy show. Yan and I didn't get it. People had lost their parents, spouses, and children, and it was not funny at all. Maybe if I had come to get a message from my grandmother who had died twenty years ago at the age of 90 and if she was joking with me from the other side, it would have been funny then. But in our condition and state of mind, we just did not get it. We were so disappointed, and Alina didn't come through that night.

John Edwards, another well-known psychic, medium, and author, happened to be doing one of his shows in Pittsburgh soon after. Edward's broad appeal has led to numerous international tours in Australia and the UK and guest appearances on everything from CNN's *Larry King Live* to *The Today Show* and *Oprah*.

I decided to give it another shot and bought tickets for his show. Yan supported me in every decision without question.

The auditorium was packed. About seven hundred people came to see Edwards, hoping to hear from their loved ones. We didn't get a message, but we were thrilled by the work that John presented. He was a very knowledgeable and intelligent man expressing his compassion for people who happened to get a reading. The messages coming from the other side were remarkable. There was no way he could have made them up. He was giving people hope and helping lighten their grief. We witnessed real communication between the deceased and their families in the auditorium. People were overwhelmed with their emotions, and we could easily relate to them. Both Yan and I could actually feel that connection. We liked Edwards a lot.

I desperately needed a private reading but was afraid to get one. I wanted to hear from my daughter, but at the same time, I was scared to hear something I wouldn't want to hear.

I found a psychic medium in the Pittsburgh area and scheduled a one-hour reading with her.

As I was getting ready for the appointment, I was doing my eyebrows and was overwhelmed with a memory of how obsessed Alina had been about her eyebrows. She had made a funny comment about mine one time. She said, "Mom, no offense, but you look like a cancer patient with your invisible eyebrows." I laughed so much and started paying more attention to my eyebrows. One day she complimented me, saying, "Good job, Mom, your eyebrows look much better now." I could not stop playing that conversation in my head and thought that, if the medium gave me a message mentioning my eyebrows, I would know it was from Alina for sure. It would be the perfect validation.

I tried not to be nervous walking into the medium's office. She asked who I wanted to communicate with and her name. Right away I did not like it. It didn't match the way John Edwards had done his readings. He didn't ask those questions and gave the names and relation status himself, and people just validated that information. In no time, I felt negative about it and didn't want to trust her.

But I told her that I wanted to connect with my daughter Alina. She then asked about her age. My insides protested, and all I could hear in my head was, "Such bullshit... I will not believe anything you say, lady."

She said she could not guarantee that my daughter would want to connect with me. Any other relatives or friends might come through though. I rolled my eyes, thinking, "Yeah sure, such a waste of time."

She closed her eyes, said some prayers, and tried to connect with the other side. I patiently waited for what would happen next.

"I have two people for you," she said, "a male and a female."

My reaction was negative again. I thought, "Who the hell is that male? I don't want any males here. I just need my daughter."

The medium asked if I recognized a tall man with green eyes. I could not think of anyone. She said he appeared to her as a strong, good-looking man who would stand out in a crowd. I could not match that description to anyone, or perhaps I simply didn't want to hear about anyone besides my daughter.

Then the medium described the female. "A petite young lady with long hair . . . her height is a little shorter than yours . . ." I got chills, and my eyes popped out. I thought, "Oh my God, no way." Then she said that her hair was light. Even lighter than mine. That was it. My disappointment reached its highest level. I said, "No, it's not my daughter. Alina had very dark hair." She then asked if Alina had ever had light hair in the past. She did. I liked that color better than the dark; I actually hated it when she dyed her hair black and always asked her to change it. The medium said maybe that's why Alina wanted to appear with her hair lighter, so I would not feel disappointed about it anymore. But to me it all sounded like bullshit.

Then the medium smiled, even slightly laughed. "Hmm, she is showing me her eyebrows, dark eyebrows. I don't know why she would do that. No other spirits have ever shown me their eyebrows."

I stopped breathing. But my disbelief remained strong. I thought that she was making everything up no matter what she said. The "eyebrow message" sounded like a shocking validation, but the light hair had messed me up from the beginning. I didn't want to believe the medium. Maybe I was not ready to receive any messages yet. The only message I probably wanted was that my daughter was waiting for me around the corner.

Then the medium said exactly what I was afraid to hear. "She says that she is not happy, but she is at peace. She does not know what to do yet. She says that she knew exactly what she was doing here, but she is not sure what she can do there."

That upset me. I cried when I got back in Yan's car and said I would never do that again. I wanted my daughter alive so badly.

I didn't want to give up though. I started reading books about how mediums actually communicate with spirits, and I learned that it was not that easy. There was a language of signs that both mediums and spirits had to learn to communicate. The spirits would show a medium a single sign that could be interpreted as something significant that could then be validated.

I finished an online mediumship video course presented by the James Van Praagh School of Mystical Arts. James Van Praagh is a well-known psychic medium and author of many books.

I learned that different mediums could have different abilities of communication. They could be clairvoyant, meaning they can see spirits. Clairsentient, having the ability to feel spirits. Clairaudient, having the ability to hear messages, either audibly or inside your mind telepathically. Claircognizant, having the ability to "just know" the information. And some could have more than just one ability that made them better communicators with the spirit world.

After becoming more knowledgeable about how mediumship works, I decided to give it another shot. One of the mediums I had been following on Facebook offered monthly reading circles. It was like a one-hour conference call where people could call in and she would give each person a reading. One evening I joined that reading circle. There were seven people there. One by one, the medium gave messages to everyone who had joined. I nervously listened to the messages she gave to the others. She finally called my name. I was the only new person in the circle; all the others had been joining every month. The medium had no idea who I was or what was happening in my life.

"Ok, Elly," she said, starting my reading. "You have been through a lot lately. They show me a water mill. It means you've been struggling so much dealing with the ups and downs, and your downs are very rough. Seems like you're dealing with a tragedy."

I just simply said, "Yes."

She continued, "I got a dad figure for you. Is your dad on the other side?"

I said, "No. But my father-in-law is."

"You must have had a very close relationship with him then. I feel the energy of a father."

I said, "Yes, we were very close."

"He is a very serious, smart, and intelligent man. He showed up wearing a very conservative black suit. He must be either Amish or Jewish."

I could not believe what she had said. The only father figure with a Jewish background who it could be was Yan's dad.

I said, "Yes, my father in-law was Jewish."

"He is saying that you're on the right path with what you're doing, and he is very proud of you. He just tipped his hat off his head. It means he bows to you."

I was speechless.

"Hmm, it does not match his serious appearance, but I hear nonstop laughing around him. I feel such bubbly energy with him."

I cried. Who else could that be other than my bubbly, silly girl with her infectious laugh?

Then the medium said, "I hear a name. Sounds like Maria."

I got chills all over my body. Maria was the name of Yan's grandma. Alina's lovely babushka who had transitioned right after Alina. I could not believe it; I was crying.

It was very nice to get a message from my father-in-law, but I desperately needed to connect with my daughter. I kept trying.

A random advertisement popped up on my Facebook. There was one company located in California that offered a psychic medium service by phone. A few mediums from California Psychics were giving a discount. I really wanted to schedule an appointment but was contemplating. I thought that they could simply google my name and get all the info about Alina. I scrolled through the pictures of their professionals, trying to find the one who might fit my needs better.

My eyes stopped at a picture of one lady who looked very kind and had such a nice, genuine smile. I read her info and got a warm feeling. She was the one. She had the ability to connect with loved ones on the other side. She had an appointment available with a waiting time of one hour. I was not sure if one hour was good enough to google my name, but I got a feeling that I could trust it.

I put my info in. And I was supposed to get a call at my scheduled time in one hour.

Two minutes later to my surprise, my phone rang. It was the lady.

I knew there was no way she could have found any info about me in two minutes. I felt very positive and open; I was ready to get a message from the other side.

The lady's voice complemented her picture. I was not disappointed in my expectations. Her tone was comforting to me. She asked my name and what I was looking for. I said that I needed to get a message from my daughter. She asked my daughter's name and when she had transitioned. Then she told me that she could not guarantee that Alina would make a connection. She explained that it was just like when we dial a number — it was not guaranteed that the person would answer your phone call. She asked me to take a deep breath and think of my daughter. Then she said a prayer and spoke.

"Alina, Alina. Pick up your phone, sweetheart, your mom wants to talk to you."

I patiently waited.

It took her a while. Then she said, "Ok, Alina is here."

I almost dropped the phone. I started shaking.

"Your daughter's age is between twenty to thirty years old. Is that right?"

"Yes, Alina is twenty."

"She is showing me a fluffy toy... it's a fluffy puppy. Does that mean anything to you?"

"Oh my God, yes, it's her dog Benji."

"She is showing me a candy. Do you know what it could mean?"

"I don't know, but her dad has a sweet tooth, and she liked buying him a special candy and always baked a special cake for him."

"Please tell your husband that his daughter is saying a special hello to him."

I could not hold back my tears.

"She is running now. Was she a runner? Did she like sports?"

"No. She never was a sporty girl. And actually, she was unable to run because of her knee injury."

"I don't know, but she keeps running. Alina, why are you running, sweetheart? Your mom does not understand."

I had no idea what it could mean. All I knew was that Alina could not run, but the lady didn't want to drop it and kept going.

"Why are you running, sweetheart? Tell us why you keep running." Then she changed her tone and said, "Oh, I see... someone is hiding around the corner. She is running AWAY. She is running away from the relationship."

With my shaky voice, I said, "Yes, that's exactly what she was doing."

"It happened very sudden. She was not sick, and she did not take her own life. She is saying that someone deliberately did that to her."

I was crying and validated her with a short "Yes."

"She is saying that she is very sorry and that she did not know that he had planned that. She is showing me a lot of police now."

"Yes, Alina was murdered." I could not stop crying.

"Oh, my goodness, Elly, I'm very sorry, I'm very sorry. Alina is dancing now. She keeps circling in her dancing, and she is smiling. And I hear some name. Marr? Mary? Maria! Alina says that Maria misses you too."

Then she said that Alina said that she loved me, but she needed to go. The medium appreciated my call and said that she was going to pray for me and my daughter. And she asked me to look at the wall right after I hung up the phone.

I hung up and looked at the wall. The foggy image of Alina's face appeared. I stared speechlessly at the wall, watching the image slowly fade away. I was in shock. For a good ten minutes, I sat without blinking or moving. I was in deep shock. And Maria had been mentioned again.

Awhile after that phone reading, Yan and I had another group reading. That one was through a Facetime call. There were other moms who had lost their children, and the medium gave a reading to each of us.

"I have a young lady," the medium said.

All the moms looked at me because they all had sons.

I got closer to the screen, and Yan stayed behind.

"She keeps playing with her hair. Her hair is long and beautiful."

"Yes, Alina loved her hair so much. She took good care of it. She would always twirl her hair during a conversation when she had to think deep."

"Are you and that man behind you together?" she asked.

"Yes, he's my husband."

"That's what I thought. Your daughter is standing between you two with her arms resting on your shoulders."

Yan nodded, and his eyes became wet.

"She is saying to tell you to stop worrying about whether she was alone when she left her body. She is saying that she had gone very quickly, and no one was waiting for her, but the angels came and lifted her up, so she was not alone. She didn't suffer and didn't even understand what had happened to her or where she was. She was very surprised, thinking, 'What the heck am I doing here?' She just said... 'Yeah, I had done something stupid.'"

The medium asked Alina if she wanted to be more specific. Then she smirked and smiled, saying, "Alina sarcastically said 'no,' and that it's none of my business and that she does not want to reveal any personal details to me."

The tone of her voice was exactly like Alina would have said it.

The medium continued, "Alina said that she had a special bond with her mom. She wants you to stop crying. She knows that the mornings are the worst, and she always tries to make you feel better and helps you to get off the bed. She wants you to know that she is at peace, but she misses you. Your daughter said it's no one's fault, and no one could have prevented it. She said it just was her time."

Then the medium asked, "Who's Maria? She is with your daughter."

Chapter 19: Signs

Odd things started happening soon after Alina passed.

I remember how shocking it was when the big portrait of Alina fell off the TV stand where we had temporarily put it before hanging it on the wall. It just randomly fell as if someone had pushed it off the stand.

We had a very nice wall clock in the dining room. It was a housewarming gift from our friends. Every hour it played a song by The Beatles, and little figures danced. One day, about six months before Alina died, the clock stopped running. Yan's uncle, a professional horologist who could repair watches and clocks, tried but was unable to fix our clock due to a complicated mechanism that required replacement parts he couldn't find anywhere. For a few months, it hung silently on the wall. One evening, a few days after the funeral, Yan and I were quietly sitting in the living room. Suddenly, we heard the music play. We both got chills. The sad strains of "Yesterday" were coming from our clock. We got silent for a moment ourselves. Then we ran to our dining room to check the clock and make sure we were not losing our minds. The clock was running. Unblinkingly, we stared at the mysterious clock and watched its figures dance to the music of the well-known song by The Beatles.

"Yesterday
All my troubles seemed so far away
Now it looks as though they're here to stay
Yesterday
Love was such an easy game to play
Now I need a place to hide away
Oh, I believe in yesterday"

*   *   *

One night, I was slowly walking upstairs, carrying my phone. I felt physically and emotionally exhausted. I could hardly breathe and had no strength to lift my legs to take the next step up. Suddenly, a voice screamed out of my phone. "Can you hear me now? Can you hear me?" It seemed the volume was at its highest. I flinched and almost dropped my phone. Despite my weakness, I bolted up the stairs and tried to shut the phone off with my shaking fingers. I sat on my bed and, with wide eyes, stared at my phone. My heart was pumping. I had no idea what had happened. I must have touched an app and started some random video.

I sat on my bed for a while and could not move. Then I opened my Facebook. To my surprise, the smiling face of Adam Lambert was the first thing that popped up. Alina knew that I was a big fan. She always laughed when I sent her pictures of him, replying, "Yes, Mom, I know he is so hot." I even wanted to go to his concert someday, but Yan obviously turned down my idea. Alina laughed, saying, "Don't worry, Mom, I'll go with you! Dad doesn't need to go with us. We can just ask him to drive us and wait."

I don't remember if Adam Lambert had ever popped up on my Facebook. Seeing his face right after having heard such an odd message from my phone intrigued me. Adam was wearing a red-hot leather jacket and holding a purple microphone. I pushed the play button and heard *"Mama."*

I immediately got chills all over my body. He was singing a song by Freddie Mercury.

"Mama, just killed a man
Put a gun against his head
Pulled my trigger, now he's dead
Mama, life had just begun
But now I've gone and thrown it all away

Mama, ooh
Didn't mean to make you cry
If I'm not back again this time tomorrow
Carry on, carry on
As if nothing really matters"

I could not believe the words he was singing to me. I couldn't stop crying. I felt the presence of my daughter so much. I could see her smiling face and could hear her voice saying, "Mama, I didn't mean to make you cry... carry on as if nothing really matters."

*   *   *

A couple weeks after we had lost Alina, I woke one morning and wanted to check my Facebook. The first thing I saw was a post by a photographer I had never heard of. He wanted to share a picture of the most vibrant rainbow (in his words) that he had ever seen. It was a double rainbow. It looked beautiful. In no time I instinctively shifted my eyes to the very top of that rainbow, hoping to see my angel daughter in the sky. And in no time, I did see her.

To my own shocking surprise, I saw the figure of my daughter's upper body. I could clearly see her face and her long hair. With her left hand, she was holding her head, tilted to the side. Two huge, white wings were visible behind that figure. I felt like I was hallucinating. Yan was awake, so I quickly shoved my phone into his hands and demanded he look and tell me if he could see Alina above the rainbow. He took a quick look and in no time said, "Yes, I see her." I immediately felt some relief. I was glad I had not lost my mind, and I was not hallucinating.

Yan said that it looked exactly like a picture Alina had sent him a couple days before she was gone—a selfie where she was holding her head with her left hand, tilted to the side. The caption was, "I'm bored."

I shared that picture on my Facebook and received many comments that other people could see her too. Later, Alina's friend's father brought this picture to our house as a gift. Yan and I both cried from such a heartfelt gesture. We put this beautiful picture in Alina's room.

Above: Photographer Dave DiCello

*   *   *

When we had moved into our new house, Alina had wanted her room to be painted purple. Now, because purple is also the color for domestic violence awareness, purple had automatically become a sign from Alina. Purple was everywhere. It felt as though she was constantly trying to remind us of her.

Alina's birthday, 7/7/97, meant that her lucky number had to be 77. Along with purple, that number had become another sign from Alina. It was everywhere. Whenever Yan and I were driving, a car with a plate with 77 on it somewhere would be in front of us. A triple 7 or 7797 was like an extra special sign that always made us pause. Whenever we parked, a car next to us had 77 in its plate number. If we happened to park and there was not a car with 77 next to us, I would disappointedly ask Alina, "Hello, why aren't you here?" And believe it or not, when we came back, there would always be a car with 77 next to us.

Seeing 77 had become our norm. We would always smile and say, "Hi, dochka." I was sitting on our deck, staring at the sky one day, talking to her, and I asked how she was going to give me her 77 sign if I was not in a car and there were no cars around. A couple minutes later, I received a text message from my friend. She sent me a picture of a car driving in front of her. It had a 77.

Whenever I had a very bad day, all my paperwork, bank balances, statements, or invoices oddly had a bunch of 7s in them. And the oddest thing was that a couple months before Alina was gone, my son had changed the plate number of his car. He made it read A777777 and explained to us that was an angel number.

One evening, I was walking around our neighborhood, pushing Angelina in a stroller. I was very upset that Alina could not enjoy spending time with her little niece. I knew how happy

Alina would have been. I walked slowly and asked her to give me a sign that she knew I was babysitting Angelina and could see us. The street was empty—no people, no cars. It was very quiet. Then a van passed me and stopped at one of our neighbor's houses. I knew it had to do with something that I had just asked for and rushed to the van to take a closer look. I was shocked by what I saw. It was a flower delivery van. It said Angels Floral & Gifts. The phone number contained 77 and 2017, the year Angelina was born. It was all written in purple, and there was a very cute picture of a little angel girl in a cute white gown holding a beautiful bouquet of flowers. I got chills and cried.

*   *   *

Every day after Yan picked me up from work, we would pick up Angelina from her babysitter. That was very tough. I cried almost every time while looking at this precious baby in our car taking the seat where Alina used to sit. My heart was breaking for my daughter because she was not part of our family anymore. I smiled at Angelina with joy that she had come into our lives, yet at the same time I cried for my daughter who was missing.

One time while driving, Angelina pointed her little finger to the empty seat next to Yan. I was sitting in the back next to Angelina. Without blinking, she stared at that empty seat, pointing to it. I shifted my eyes back and forth from her little finger to the empty sit in front of me, trying to figure out what was she pointing at. There was nothing that could possibly have caught her attention. Then she laughed as if someone was making a funny face trying to make her laugh. While joyfully laughing, she clapped her hands and slapped her chubby legs. To me, it seemed like someone was playing with her. That was such a breathtaking scene to watch. My eyes met Yan's in the rearview mirror. His undoubted look confirmed my thought that our daughter was in the car with us.

Another day, Angelina was at our house, waiting for her parents to pick her up. Yan lay on the floor, playing with Angelina, and I sat on the couch, watching them. Angelina was about eight or nine months and was only able to produce separate sounds. Yan was helping her make a pyramid, and she seemed to be concentrating on her work. Suddenly she raised her little head and turned to the wall where Alina's big portrait was. She stuck her little tongue out and slowly said, "Allliiina."

I held my breath and nervously looked at Yan. His wide eyes asked me if I had heard what Angelina said. And just to stop our doubt, Angelina pointed her little finger to Alina's portrait and slowly said, "Allliiina," again. Yan and I could not believe what had just happened. When the kids showed up, I told them about it, but they didn't believe us. Artem asked his daughter to say "Alina" again, but she just ignored him. Since then, I have asked my granddaughter to say Alina's name so many times, but she never has.

*   *   *

Aside from the physical signs of her presence, my feelings could suddenly change for no reason. A short while after Alina was gone and the ugly feelings clung to me like a wet blanket, I noticed something very weird happening to me. I was in my office, feeling miserable. I was angry, scared, and upset all at once. I was trying to hold myself together and just do my work. Suddenly, I felt love and peace fill my mind and body. I got very confused. I could not explain why I felt that. I hated the whole world; I hated the fact that my daughter was gone; I hated myself and everything around me. In my present condition, I could not love anything or anyone. Yet suddenly, I was overwhelmed with the feeling of love. I could not understand where it came from or how it was even possible to feel peace and love when my daughter was dead, my heart was broken, and my entire being was shattered. That feeling didn't last long, but it made me feel calmer for the rest of the day.

The next day, I happened to read an article where a father shared his experiences of connecting with his deceased daughter. He described exactly what I had felt the previous day. He said that his daughter tried to integrate her energy into his so he could feel her presence and love. That wowed me. I didn't get that sudden feeling of love very often, but when I did, I was no longer confused. I knew it was my daughter trying to integrate her loving energy with me. Those acts of such beautiful integration helped me get through the most difficult of days.

Synchronicity soon became my norm too. In the beginning, it was very odd when I noticed that my thoughts and conversations were being repeated by other people, as if my questions were being answered through books, TV, Facebook, or other people saying random things. Facebook was especially weird. Random stuff was always popping up and oddly matching the events of that day. I could have a conversation with my friends, discussing some sensitive topic, and a random picture or a quote related to that topic would pop up. What I was eating, saying, seeing, or hearing would always pop up on my Facebook feed later. It really felt as if I was being watched and told, "I know what you're doing."

At first, I thought it was a weird coincidence. But those things happened every day, and it was too obvious and impossible to ignore. After having visited a dentist, I scrolled through my Facebook, wondering what I might see related to that. I expected a picture of someone's big smile showing their teeth or a toothpaste commercial or an advertisement for a dentist's office. But what popped up on my Facebook made me laugh. One woman had shared a picture of bloody dental tools, and they looked identical to the tools that my doctor had used working on my mouth. Why that woman had shared such a disgusting picture, I had no idea, but I knew that it was a message just for me. "Don't doubt it, Mom, I do know you went to the dentist."

All these messages were unique and often very funny. They matched Alina's personality. And every time I received them, it would give me those chills that made me feel her presence.

One evening, Yan and I were quietly sitting in the living room with no desire to even talk to each other. We both were very down and overwhelmed by our grief. We wanted to watch a movie but could not find anything that fit the state of our minds. I grabbed my phone, and the first thing I saw on my Facebook was a comment by a grieving mom saying she had watched *The Shack* and it had helped her understand her grief better. I immediately asked Yan to order that movie on Netflix. The movie was about a father whose youngest daughter was kidnapped and murdered and how he dealt with his grief and all that was associated with that event, feelings, and emotions. The storyline resonated with our reality. Yan cried like a child during the whole movie; he felt that father with every fiber of his being.

The father had met God and other spiritual beings. They had helped him go through his grief and deep depression by revealing important truths that had transformed his understanding of his tragedy and had changed his life forever. We needed such a movie that night, and it had been given to us. When the movie was over, Yan wiped his tears and, looking at Alina's portrait on the wall, said, "What a movie. Thank you, baby." The spotlights in the room flickered then. They flickered twice.

When Yan and I still had a hard time going to crowded places and preferred staying home, some random post on Facebook, unrelated to anything, caught my attention. It was a very bright purple flyer advertising an upcoming show at one of Pittsburgh's theaters that I had never even heard of. The design of the flyer mesmerized me. It had big beautiful eyes that stared at me. They looked like Alina's eyes. Right underneath was written, "Next to Normal," the name of the show. The design reminded me of the design of Alina's headstone. I got very curious about that theater and bought tickets to the show.

The theater looked very different from other theaters I had been in—a compact auditorium with a moving platform instead of a stage. There were only four rows of seats all around the platform. We didn't expect to be engulfed in such an intimate atmosphere at such a unique theater.

Four actors took their places on the platform, playing out a family scene. Mom, Dad, and their two grown-up children. The story unfolded through beautiful singing and acting. The mother was suffering a deep depression; she had attempted suicide and was seeking psychiatric help. The husband was trying to help his wife, and the daughter and son were trying to talk to their mom and explain some life things too. Unexpectedly, we realized that the son was just the spirit of their child whom they had lost eighteen years ago, and the daughter had been born a year after he passed and had never met her brother. The son had always been a part of his mom's life, but he never existed in the lives of the others. The mom always saw her boy and talked to him, and the rest of the family thought she had lost her mind. They convinced her to get treatment to get rid of those thoughts so their family could have a normal life again.

We cried the whole time, wondering how in the world we had ended up watching a story that resonated with our life, which was so unimaginable for others. There was one scene where my heart just screamed. The mom had finally agreed to get a procedure that would erase her memory so she could forget her son and move on. She was at the clinic in a patient's gown, still debating whether to get the treatment. Her family was convincing her to do so, and the son was running around screaming not to get rid of him. "I'm here, Mom. I am alive, I'm alive, I'm alive." And he was wearing a purple shirt.

It was such a beautiful and profound performance. The mom shook me to the core. It felt as if the actress had really lost her child and knew exactly how that felt. It didn't look as if she was playing; it felt like she was living that scene. And the actor who played the spirit son made the presence of my own daughter feel so real.

Despite receiving the treatment, the mom still remembered her son. She had forgotten everything else, but her son could not be erased. The rest of her family had opened up their hearts and started seeing the son too. The story ended with the family agreeing to make their life next to normal. They knew they could not be a normal family anymore, but they wanted to make it as close to normal as possible. Yan and I needed to see that show as part of our grieving process. I haven't seen any other flyers from that theater anywhere again.

* * *

Holidays were the hardest to handle. It was too painful to stay home on Christmas, so I booked a little getaway vacation with Artem and his family. We were going to Myrtle Beach, SC. During the whole drive there, I felt the presence of a guardian angel. I asked myself if I was making it up. The feeling of his presence was very strong, and I could not deny it. I quietly sat in the passenger's seat, trying not to let Yan know that I was distracted by such a strange feeling.

I felt the presence of a big dude with a long beard and mustache. He wore a long coat with a belt tied under his big belly. I felt as if our car had been wrapped in his strong arms, protecting us from any possible damage like an impermeable bubble that anything coming toward our car would bounce off of. I felt very safe and secure. But I felt very uncomfortable revealing this feeling to Yan. I started telepathically talking to that being. I asked him if he was our guardian angel. I immediately felt his answer as a "yes." I asked where Alina was. He telepathically said that Alina was very busy taking care of other important things and had asked him to be our guardian angel during our travel time. He felt like a very kind and funny guy. I asked what his name was and was very intrigued by the answer given to me.

"Robert" was clearly imprinted in my mind. I smirked as I talked to myself. "Robert? Seriously? Who the heck is Robert?" That name didn't sound familiar. And if I was making it up, I probably would have chosen some other name that I knew better. Just to be sure that I was not making it up, I asked one more time what his name was. No other names other than Robert felt right to me. So Robert was our guardian angel whom our daughter had sent to protect us while we traveled. It made me smile. I was overwhelmed by the amazing feeling of being connected with the universe, and I could not hide it.

Yan looked at me suspiciously and asked if I was ok. I couldn't stay quiet any longer. I asked him not to think I was crazy and revealed what I had been feeling. My husband had gotten used to my stories and didn't think I had lost my mind. He just softly smiled and pointed to the car passing us: 77 was on its plate.

We parked at the hotel garage, and while Yan unloaded the car, I crazily shifted my eyes from one car to another through the whole garage looking for a 77. I was disappointed by not seeing any. I got a little upset, thinking Alina must have been really busy. As we approached the hotel entrance, I almost jumped when I saw a car parked right next to the entrance: 777 was excitedly screaming at me, "Hello, Mother! Don't you worry. I am here!"

We got to our room, and Artem turned on the TV. Shocked, he said, "Mom, look." There was a commercial showing the number 777-7777. It was not shocking to me though; it confirmed one more time that Alina was with us.

"Did you see the car with a crown that was parked at the entrance?" Kate asked me. I had missed that car but was so excited to hear about another sign from my daughter.

I could not get "Robert" out of my mind and tried to find that name somewhere as a validation to my car experience, but such a name had not been found anywhere in the hotel, so I stopped looking and almost forgot about it.

Two days later, we went to a pirate show. We parked at the theater, and there was our favorite 77 on a car nearby. At the entrance, we were greeted by a crew in purple outfits. We took our seats in row A. Dinner would be served during the show. I looked at the tag on our table and was speechless. It said, "Thank you. Your server's name is ROBERT." I silently looked at Yan to check if he had seen the tag yet and met his wide eyes expressing, "Oh my God, I did see it."

The show started. A big pirate ship was the stage. The main character, a young pirate girl, appeared at the top of the ship. She had a petite, beautifully built body. Her hair was dark, perfectly straight, and long. Her eyes seemed dark too. Her grace gave me chills. She could have been my daughter's twin. A pirate captain joined the scene. He was a big dude with a long beard and mustache. And he was wearing a long coat with a belt tied under his big belly.

Chapter 20: Spiritual Walk

A very nice trail stretched all along the river just steps away from my office. Every day I would take a walk during lunch time. The trail was always busy. People were walking, running, biking, or walking their dogs. The weird thing was that the animals and birds started acting oddly toward me. One bird suddenly flew out of nowhere to cross the road right in front of my face. Another bird did a little dance, flying in circles right above my head, and then quickly flew away. One time, as I was walking, some weird bird was flying very low toward me, about to cause a head-on collision. And if I hadn't tilted my head to the side, it would have hit me. Another time, a butterfly flew right next to me, acting like it was my walking partner.

The squirrels always made noises, trying to get my attention. They were not afraid of me and always stared into my eyes. A squirrel came out of the bushes one day and ran toward me. I stopped and reached out my hand while the squirrel looked very deep into my eyes and almost let me pet it.

The birds' and other animals' behavior was unlike normal animal behavior. I read in one of my books that spirits could play with the energies of low-vibrating creatures and make them act in a way that would get our attention. This was one of their ways of letting us know they were here. Knowing that my daughter was making these birds and animals act weird always made me smile.

Sometimes it was way too funny, and I could not hold back my laughing, saying, "Alina, seriously?" One day there was a goofy raccoon running around. The other day, I saw a little animal sticking its head out of a hole. I stopped to take a picture of it. Suddenly it came out of the hole completely, quickly peed, and went back into the hole. I laughed so much.

A lot of people seemed to be wearing purple shirts all the time, too, as if no other color was permitted on the trail. They had tied their shoes with bright purple shoelaces, and their dogs had purple leashes. At first it seemed like I was losing my mind. I remembered one day I was walking with my head spinning around, thinking, "What the heck is going on?" As I kept walking, I asked my daughter, "Alina, is it you who's making all of this?"

"Oh yeah, sure," I heard a loud answer from the guy who was passing me and talking on the phone.

Every day I walked the same way, and every time I got different signs. One day it was a puddle shaped as a heart. Another day I saw a lock with a heart attached to a bridge that I crossed on my way. Hearts were literally everywhere in the sky and on the ground. One day I saw "I love you" written in chalk, and another day it was "You are doing great" with a smiley face.

I remember one day I was not feeling great at all, and while walking I asked, "Where are you, dochka? Just tell me please where you are." Then I looked straight, and there was a big purple arrow on an electric pole. The arrow was pointing to the sky, pointing to where my daughter was. I started crying. I lost the desire to walk and turned around to go back to the office. Then I got an urge to turn back and walk a little farther. I did. On my way, there was a little rock, a colorful rock with a painted sun and the word "shine" written on it. I picked it up and brought it back to my office. I knew it was a present from my daughter, my beautiful shining light.

Every day I was so excited to take my spiritual walk and connect with my daughter. I could not wait for lunch time. I had such an unexplainable feeling that she was waiting for me there. The moment I stepped on the trail, I would say, "Hi, dochka, I am here." My daughter would give me different signs or telepathically answer my questions. Some days she just silently walked beside me, and I could feel her soft tiny hand holding mine.

*   *   *

One day when I had stepped on the trail right after saying "hello" to my daughter, my mind got very loud. It felt like there was a parade going on. Suddenly, I felt the presence of so many people marching and carrying flags. They were loud. My daughter was leading the crowd.

She was laughing and excitingly saying, "Oh my God, Mom, I am on a special mission with my friends now. We came down for six days to visit our moms and let them know we are here. You're the first one whom we have visited because I told my friends that you're so easy to connect with. Good job, Mom, you have figured it out. But other moms have not, so I can't stay long. I have to go. See you later, Mom." Then it became quiet. I could not believe what I had experienced. It felt so real and had made me happy.

*   *   *

Alina happened to celebrate her last birthday in Miami while visiting her friend Val, who had been her roommate during her first year on the Greensburg campus. Zach, her other roommate, had been traveling with Alina at that time, and his birthday was just a day before Alina's. So they celebrated their 20th together in Miami.

One day on my spiritual walk, Alina told me not to forget to wish Zach a happy birthday. It was just a week before Alina's 21st. I felt like she wanted me to buy a gift for him. Right after work, Yan and I went shopping. I bought a gift card and picked a very nice birthday card. One side of the card had a purple strap with colorful polka dots. I thought it was perfectly associated with Alina. Yan needed to buy some stuff at the liquor store, so I joined him. He went to his favorite area where the vodka was stored, and my mouth dropped when I saw a bottle that had never been there before.

The bottle was wrapped in a colorful label that was just like the picture Alina had taken at The Walls park in Miami that had also been used as a design for her memory t-shirt. I had never seen that vodka before. It said Three Olives, and there was a little crown right in the middle. I was mesmerized and stared at that bottle for a few minutes. I remembered I had laughed at the picture she sent me from Miami where the three of them were standing at the wall. Alina was in the middle, and she looked so little compared to her friends. I knew right away Alina wanted me to buy this bottle for Zach's 21st birthday.

The next day I was on the trail, and to my surprise there was a hotel key card lying in the middle of the path as if someone had intentionally placed it there. The card was purple and had colorful polka dots on it. It looked identical to the card I bought for Zach. I picked it up. Without any doubt I knew it was Alina saying thank you and that she liked the gift. In fact, that vodka has never been displayed in the store since that day.

*   *   *

A few parking lots were along the trail, and I always saw at least one car with a 77 plate number there. If something unusual happened during my walk—like construction with a big truck blocking my way or a big excavator digging—I knew it would have a 77 on it. I always smiled after checking it out and finding validation for my feeling of knowing.

One day, the trail was unusually empty. I was the only one on the whole trail. I found it very strange. I walked on a quiet trail, trying to connect with Alina. She was quiet too. She was not saying "hello" to me. I got upset and disappointed by not being able to make a connection. When I was almost to the point where I usually turn to go back, I was still alone with no one passing me or approaching me. Suddenly, I heard a motorcycle behind me. It was getting louder and louder. I turned around and saw a policeman riding a motorcycle. That was so strange. Who would ride a motorcycle on a trail when there was a road right next to it? I stepped aside to give him space to pass. I didn't even look at him. Surprisingly I heard a loud "Hello, ma'am."

I looked around and saw another policeman on his motorcycle. He said, "Hello, ma'am," too and wished me a good day. A few more passed me. I instinctively counted them. There were seven. I kept walking as they passed. Then, a big crowd of teenagers were riding their bicycles, and almost every single one said, "Hello, ma'am." "Good morning, ma'am." I stood at the side of the path, and tears ran down my face as I said "hello" back to all those kids. It felt like my daughter didn't want me to be upset or disappointed. She made a quiet trail loud again and had brought a bunch of "hellos" to me.

This trail had become a part of my life, and it was a vital therapy for my grieving process. The days when the connection did not happen brought me to a very dark place. To keep going on with life, I needed to stay connected with my daughter all the time. The moment I was back in the office I immediately called Yan and shared my stories about the walk. And every day he waited for that call because it helped him breathe and move through his day, too.

Chapter 21: Writing to my Daughter

I have learned that we can communicate with spirits through our writing. You can write your questions on a piece of paper, a spirit can put the answers into your mind, and then you can write them down. I had hesitated to do so because I was always nervous, and my mind was very busy. To let a spirit put their thoughts into your mind, you had to make it free from your own thoughts first. I was not sure if I could put my racing thoughts behind me and was afraid of being disappointed by writing something that sounded like I had just made it up.

One day, when I didn't feel much anxiety and my mind was not racing much, I was brave enough to try to write. I was supposed to write a question to my daughter and then the answer to it, the first thing that came to mind. I was not supposed to think about my answer or judge it. I took a few deep breaths and started writing. I tried my best to stay as relaxed as possible and not think. When I was done, my writing looked like this:

Hello, sweetheart.

Hi, Mom.

What are you doing?

Watching over you.

What does it even mean?

Making sure you're ok.

But I'm not ok, I miss you, I need you here.

I'm here too.

I don't see you.

You see me in pictures.

That's not enough.

Deal with that.

You're so mean.

You're so annoying.

It made me laugh when I read that conversation. It was not exactly what I wanted to hear. I wanted to hear how much my daughter loved and missed me. But what had come out of my mind sounded exactly like Alina with her funny attitude.

Alina didn't like my tendency to talk about the same things repeatedly. Whenever I had an issue with her or any others, I tended to complain and explain things, repeating them a few times. Alina always gave me a look, saying, "Mom, we got it the first time, ok." But I would still talk about it despite her warning me to stop, and she would give me a dirty look, saying how annoying I was because one time would never be enough for me. That look always made me realize that I was too much with my smart talking, and I would shut my mouth then.

There was no doubt that those words had come from my daughter; they were not my own thoughts for sure. I felt like she had given me that dirty look again because she had gotten annoyed with my crying and asking for signs all the time even though she was constantly giving me them. I read my writing and laughed. I apologized to her for not being appreciative of her hard work trying to give me signs all the time.

I was working in my office another day. Suddenly I felt overwhelmed with a very warm feeling of love. I felt the presence of my daughter very strongly. I felt her arms wrapping around my neck from behind. I closed my eyes to enjoy the feeling and put my hands on my shoulders so I could feel her. As I was holding her hands, she said that I should get a piece of paper, relax, not think, and just write. I quickly grabbed a pen.

"Mom, hello. I'm here next to your right side. I like all your pictures in the office. Angelina is beautiful... I watch over her all the time. She knows me. She talks with me very often, and so does Benji. We play when you're at work. I miss you, but I'm having fun here. Lots of friends and teachers. I laugh all the time."

Then I asked her when my time was because I was tired of being here without her.

"Your time is not soon. You have to finish your book and help other grieving parents. You're doing everything right in the way I guide you. You haven't gotten lost. You've figured everything out. You came to earth to get your experiences and grow. When you get back here, you will be amazed with your growth. You will be proud of how you've changed. I'm not going back to earth any time soon because I was so busy down there and just want to relax and enjoy myself up here now."

Then I said that I was so sad she didn't have any kids and never experienced being a mom.

"I have so many kids from my other lives. They are all with me now."

144

Then in my mind I saw her being in a very bright, colorful field with flowers. She was smiling and running around with a few kids next to her. There was a dog there. A big chocolate dog was running around the field, playing with them. I expressed a feeling of surprise. And my hand had written, *"It's my dog, Mom. His name is Bernard."*

One of my coworkers came into my office, and I got disconnected then. I had read my writing a few times after and thought about how Alina had always talked about getting a big dog one day. She loved Benji dearly, but she always wanted to have a big dog in her own house. And she always talked about her future children and how much she already loved them and could not wait to take care of them. I googled a brown dog, and Bernard popped up right away. It was a picture of a Boykin spaniel. A beautiful chocolate-colored dog with long curly-haired ears. That dog stared at me from the Google website. He looked right into my eyes and smiled. And there was a very bright light shining at his smiling mouth.

I did not feel comfortable sharing my experiences with other people. But it just happened that one of Alina's best friends had become a very important person whom I felt like sharing all my stories with. Becca was very close to Alina, and they had spent so much time together, sharing good and bad moments of their lives. Becca had been Alina's roommate during her time at college in Greensburg. Also, she was one of Alina's friends who had lived in that house in Oakland and witnessed the horror of that night when Alina's life had been taken away. I always felt that Alina wanted me to tell Becca about all the signs I was getting. I felt that it was very important and vital for her grieving process too.

Every time I shared my story with Becca, she would respond with an exciting "Oh my God" message, saying that it was exactly what Alina would say or do. She knew my daughter very well. It was comforting and exciting to me that Becca would always confirm Alina's words and actions in these signs. Becca had no doubt that it was her best friend letting her know that she was still here watching over us.

Chapter 22: Forgiveness

My family felt so much anger and hatred toward Darby. All of Alina's friends did too. I believe those feelings were the automatic response of a normal human being knowing what had happened to such a beautiful and innocent girl.

Yan and I were mad with the desire of making his family suffer too. Their son had turned our lives into ruins, and because his family lived in a different state, the people around them were probably not aware that this family had raised a murderer. We wanted to reveal the story of what their monster son had done and make them ashamed.

I wanted his mother to be humiliated for giving birth to such a monster who had destroyed my child. I wanted his father to suffer for the rest of his life for bailing his predator son out of jail and giving him a green light to kill my daughter. But despite our urge to make that family suffer, we never took any action that would have brought us down to Darby's level.

We knew nothing would ever bring our daughter back. I remember having nonstop conversations with my son about love, hate, and harm. He agreed that harm only creates more harm and that our souls could not be healed from harm. The healing could come from love only. I felt as though my soul was constantly talking to me. I repeated to my family that Darby had made his own choice and had to be responsible for his own actions. The voice in my mind kept saying, "Don't worry . . . he will be taken care of. It's not your job . . . do not harm yourself." And I kept telling my son and my husband that justice would take care of Darby. Life would take care of him and his family, and we should be focused on how to take care of ourselves.

Darby did not deserve to be the focus of our lives. He had never been a part of our lives, and we decided to just let it go. Instead of hate for him and his family, we wanted to fill our hearts with love for our beautiful girl and to focus on keeping her memory alive. We were able to stop the desire for revenge.

Later on, my spiritual knowledge, my spiritual experiences, and my connection with my daughter had replaced the feeling of hate for Darby with a feeling of pity for his soul. I felt like he was a victim too. I realized that he was a victim of his own mind, and he was seeking help. What he did to my daughter was a wrong choice that he thought would lead to the survival of his soul. He must have been hurting so much. Rejection is one of the most hurtful feelings the human mind can endure. I'm sure his soul was trying to tell him that he should go through that painful experience and come out of it a stronger person. He must have been disconnected from his soul. He must have been too weak to fight his ego.

Darby's ego had convinced him to make a wrong decision in taking an action that he thought would prove to the world that he mattered on this earth. But he already mattered. Every soul matters on earth, and my daughter knew that. She knew his soul was seeking help, and she wanted to help. She knew he was disconnected from a source of light, and that's why his soul had been stuck in darkness. She saw that not enough light had pushed him to do the wrong things in life. By giving her love, compassion, and understanding, she tried to bring him closer to the light. My daughter didn't want to give up on him but had finally realized that his ego would never let him come out of the darkness, and it was pulling her away from the light too. She tried to disconnect from his ego then so her own soul could survive. But his ego didn't let her escape. His darkness had engulfed her body. My daughter's body may not have survived, but her light has never dimmed.

I felt that her light still wanted to help his tortured soul. I felt that my daughter felt pity for him and the choice he made. She imprinted her thoughts onto my mind, saying that he couldn't go back yet. "His soul is not ready to go back. He needs to stay alive and think about what he has done. He needs to learn his lesson so his soul can evolve before it returns home. He would be in so much trouble, Mom. He already has been and still is. Please let him stay alive. He really needs to."

I was very confused by those thoughts, but I could not shut off my mind from talking to me. I felt what my daughter might have been feeling for him. I was not angry; I didn't hate him; I felt pity for him. I felt pity for what he had done to himself. He could have enjoyed his life, been a famous basketball player, been a husband and a father, but instead, his ego had chosen to lock himself in prison. I felt a lot of pity for both, for my daughter and for him. I felt so mad at the world that it had thrown that young couple into life circumstances with such a tragic outcome for both sides. My heart was breaking that the world hadn't let the circumstances turn out differently so both could have survived that life challenge.

I didn't hate his parents anymore. I felt sorry for them too. I could feel their broken hearts. I'm sure they had done everything possible to help their son's soul. And I am sure it was not the life they had planned for their son either.

I shared my feelings with Yan, and he sarcastically advised me not to share it with other people. He said I would be locked up in a psychiatric clinic. I agreed that it was very odd to feel pity for the person who had brutally murdered my daughter. But I could not help that feeling. I looked at the situation with the eyes of my soul. And I looked much deeper into it. I had seen the bigger picture. From a soul perspective, I felt very sad and had pity for everyone who involved in that heartbreaking story.

All this happened before we ever went to trial.

I mentioned to Yan that I wished we had not gone for the death penalty. I told him that I had changed my mind, and if we ever had the chance to rethink our decision, I would go for a life sentence instead of the death penalty. But the process had taken its turns, and we were not the ones making justice. A jury selection day had already been scheduled. The process was going very slowly, and the constant postponements were very disappointing. I worried about the trial, and the anticipation was overwhelming.

A few days after I had shared my odd feelings with Yan, I suddenly got overwhelmed with the feeling of love while working in my office. I felt that I needed to write again. I took a pen, took a few deep breaths trying to calm my thoughts, and wrote.

"Hi, Mom. Relax. You worry too much. I'm OK. Everything is simple. Darby is a piece of crap. He will be done soon."

My first thought after I read that message was that Darby would get killed in jail. I went on my spiritual walk. Right in the middle of the path, there was a knife. A big stainless-steel kitchen knife. That would be the last thing I thought someone could possibly lose on a walking trail. I got chills, thinking, "Oh my God, is he really going to die so we won't have to go to trial then?" Then I saw a car parked by the trail. The plate said DEAD HEAD. I called Yan the next minute and told him that something was supposed to happen.

Within thirty minutes of getting back to the office, I received an email from our attorneys advising us that we might have some changes regarding the trial, and it needed to be discussed. There was the option that Darby would plead guilty and immediately be sentenced to life in prison. A trial would not be needed then. I could not believe such a quick turn of the process. That was exactly what I had been wishing for lately. I wanted the case closed. I desperately wanted it to be over so I could focus on my daughter and all the beautiful things we had been doing in her honor. I was not sure if my husband and my son would be satisfied with a life sentence for Darby though. We had a family talk and discussed all the pros and cons.

My son needed more time to think, and I wanted to confirm with Alina if we were doing the right thing. So we decided not to rush our decision and see how we felt in a couple of days. I asked Alina to give me a sign as a simple "yes" or "no." For the next two days, I looked for that sign everywhere. All my sources stayed quiet. No signs on Facebook, nothing on TV, nothing in my books; even my trail was quiet. I had almost given up, but my daughter never disappointed me.

I was walking on the trail, the same way as usual. Everything looked the same as the day before. Then I saw something that shook me to the core. There was a huge advertising banner right across the road along the trail. From time to time, the picture on the banner would change. What had appeared in front of my eyes and was cheerfully screaming at me had not been there yesterday. They must have just replaced the old banner with a new one. It was a very colorful picture advertising a summer vacation at some resort. It said **"YES let's go."** I got chills, and my body started shaking. Yes, my daughter wanted us to go for a life sentence. I took a picture of it and sent it to my guys with the following comment: "Here is a confirmation from Alina." I got the same response from everyone as "Yes, let's go."

My family went for a life sentence for Darby. We were not going to face a trial, and the day of the sentencing had been scheduled quickly. Even though Darby had not died in jail, he would somehow be done with it soon as my daughter had said. He was going to prison much sooner than expected.

Chapter 23: Sentencing

The year after Alina's death had been the most challenging year of our lives. We were approaching the one-year anniversary of our family tragedy. Despite my spiritual knowledge, experiences, and new beliefs, the devastation was overwhelming. The memories of the scariest day of my life were still very fresh. The panic attacks still kicked in pretty often, and my whole being had been devastated by the loss of my beautiful child. I was scared to wake up on October 8th again. I didn't know what to expect.

My son's and his wife's birthdays were approaching as well. It felt inadequate, inappropriate, amoral, and heartbreaking to wish them "Happy Birthday" on the day that my daughter had been murdered. I knew my family was never going to be the same.

I sat at Alina's grave for so long the day before the anniversary. I was remembering every single moment of the last day she was alive. I thought about everything she had done and every word she had said on her last day of being on earth with her loving family. I still could not believe what had happened to my daughter and to our family. As I cried silently, I told Alina how one year had passed and what I had done and how much I had changed.

Suddenly I got the feeling that someone was staring at me. I looked straight ahead and noticed a chipmunk on top of a headstone thirty feet away. It looked directly at me. I got the urge to get up and approach it. The cute little animal got scared of me and ran away, but when I looked at the headstone it had been sitting on, I lost my breath. My daughter had given me a very beautiful sign. There was a little purple rock that said **Love you, Mom!** I asked Yan to come over and look. The moment he saw the rock, he cried. We both missed our little girl and were devastated that we would have to spend the rest of our lives without seeing her beautiful face or hearing her infectious laugh.

In the late morning of October 8th, our family and friends gathered at Alina's grave and had a small memorial ceremony that was followed by a memorial dinner at our house. All of Alina's friends were welcome to join us too. Late in the evening, everybody went to the Greenburg campus for the lantern release that had been organized by the director of the Outdoor Adventure & Community Service where Alina had lived during her time at Pitt-Greensburg and had been its vice president during her last semester before moving to Oakland.

The night of the lantern release was warm and peaceful. No wind touched the leaves on the trees. The lanterns floated smoothly up to the sky, the beautiful place where my daughter was. The realization that our daughter was gone hit so hard, but acknowledging that she was loved and remembered soothed the pain.

To my own surprise, I handled the first anniversary much better that I had expected I would. I was glad I had overcome another unknown and heart-wrenching first-after-Alina-was-gone event, and now I knew what to expect next year. It was time to get ready for the day of the sentencing.

We were informed that any family member or friend could make a victim impact statement at the sentencing and that either

Yan or I should make one too. I freaked out, thinking there was no way I would be able to stand in front of the crowd and speak. My insides protested the fact that I would have to face Darby and speak in front of him. I was afraid of how I might react in the courtroom. Artem refused to speak as well, so Yan agreed to make the statement from the family. I could not wait until that day would be over. The anticipation made me sick to my stomach.

I got a few messages from Alina's friends informing me that they were going to make statements at the sentencing and how important it was for them. And just a few days before the day of the verdict, I got a very strong feeling that I had to make my own statement. I got the urge to face Darby, tell him how wrong his decision was, and reveal how much Alina had cared for him and had believed in him. I knew my daughter wanted me to deliver her last words to him.

I had always struggled with public presentations and writing essays. I knew that someone would definitely need to help me, but the voice inside of my head convinced me that I would be OK, and I knew exactly what should be said. The presence of my daughter felt very strong. It felt like she was using my body to express her feelings. In two days, my victim impact statement was ready. I felt confident in presenting it. Those words were the words of my daughter, and I would be responsible for delivering them to the world. My son decided to say a few words to Darby too.

On the morning of October 17th, just nine days after the one-year anniversary of our daughter's death, our family and friends gathered at the door of the courtroom. The atmosphere was intense. Finally, the door opened, and everyone proceeded inside. There was not one empty seat. To our surprise there was a whole section of police officers also seated in the room. I asked Yan if Darby was that dangerous that so much police force was necessary. Later, we learned that all of them were off-duty that morning and had come just to support our daughter. I was very touched.

No one from Darby's family was present.

The judge proceeded into the courtroom, and Darby was brought before the judge. He did not act the way he had at the preliminary hearing. His head was down, and his body language expressed his understanding of what was happening. He did not look like a murderer. He didn't look like a monster. He presented himself as a nice, soft-spoken person. My mother-in-law asked Yan who was answering the judge's questions, and her eyes widened when she was told that Darby was speaking. She said she did not expect him to have such a pleasant voice. Darby quietly answered "yes" to all of the judge's questions and said out loud that he was guilty. My insides screamed, "Why would you need to do that?"

Ten of Alina's friends took their turns speaking to the judge and expressing how the murder of their friend had impacted their lives. They all were emotional and expressed so much anger and hatred to Darby. They all were grief-stricken and heartbroken. But only one of them had witnessed Alina lying in a pool of her own blood.

It was Zack, Becca's boyfriend, who happened to stay at the house that night. A young man who looked unfamiliar to me that morning and whom I felt so much for and cared for now. My heart was breaking as I saw him dissolve into tears in front of the judge and express his devastation. I felt guilty for pushing him into Alina's room that morning and making him witness what had been done to her. I will never forget the horror on his face as he stared at the destroyed and unrecognizable face of his friend while her mother hysterically screamed at him to look what had been done to her daughter. He was the only one of Alina's friends who would always remember her face in a way that none of the others would ever imagine . . . And I felt guilty for forcing that on him.

Then, it was Yan's turn to present his statement.

"Hello. My name is Yan Sheykhet, and I am the proud father of Alina and Artem Sheykhet. Twenty-one years ago, we received the most precious gift from God, Alina. She was raised in a loving family and has many friends who also love her. Alina enjoyed being around people and made everyone who knew her a better person. She touched so many hearts. She loved life with every fiber of her being and wanted to make the world a better place.

"She was a very strong and smart girl and very proud of her Russian descent. Her life was filled with laughter, and she enjoyed joking around with her family and friends.

"Alina was a very talented young lady. She performed all over the state, taking the lead role in many productions.

"Because of my daughter, we have met so many good people over the years, and our house was always filled with many of her friends, not only filling her heart with love and making her life whole but ours as well.

"I had a very close relationship with my daughter. She was a very easy person to talk to, and we talked about everything as she had a broad knowledge about many topics. I have always told my kids to never give up, and she never did.

"When she informed me about her new relationship, I did not support her in that decision because I knew it would not serve her future life in the way she had planned for herself. Then when

she realized that she got into the wrong relationship, she tried to get out of it. She asked him to stop calling and texting her and removed him from her social media, and that is when he broke into her house.

"This is the moment when I feel the system had failed us due to the miscommunication between counties when they let him out of jail in September of 2017.

"I always told her people like him can hit you from behind, and that is exactly what happened. She was much stronger than him in so many ways. He is nothing more than a loser and a coward. He only had enough power to overcome my daughter, yet he did not have the courage or the guts to confront either me or my son. My anger is immeasurable. He is not a man. He is a wild animal, and I will never be able to comprehend how someone could do what he has done.

"He has taken Alina from us in an unimaginable way. I truly believe his goal was to destroy our family. The pain and loss that my family has endured in the past year is incomprehensible. He has stolen so much from us, including a future with our daughter. My family has chosen to stay strong through this, and we will not give the defendant the satisfaction of taking our lives from us as well. I loved my daughter before and will always love her.

"I feel as though his behavior is a direct reflection on how his parents raised him. He is unstable and unable to accept loss or rejection. I hope the general population in the place where he is going can help him more than his parents could.

"We are currently in the process of pushing through Alina's Law to help victims of violent crimes. We are also creating a nonprofit organization in her name. Through these efforts, her

> *memory will stay alive forever, and Alina will continue to touch people's hearts and help others as she has already done... something that she was very passionate about."*

He was nervous. He faced the judge the whole time while speaking and never looked at his daughter's murderer once. Darby stared at his back through the whole speech.

After Yan finished, the prosecutor called my name, and I joined my husband in facing the judge. My hands were shaking as I held my letter. My voice was trembling.

> *"My daughter died. It's a very short phrase. But it's strong enough to shock and paralyze every single cell of my body when I have to say that phrase. It feels like my mouth was not developed for saying that phrase out loud because my brain was not built to comprehend the meaning of that phrase.*
>
> *"My heart feels empty when I think about tomorrow. Where the bright future of my daughter was shining, there's a hole there now. No graduation (she was so proud to be a Pitt student). No dream career (she was determined to be a doctor of physical therapy). No wedding dress (she would have looked absolutely stunning wearing it). No children (Alina loved little kids and could not wait to be a mom one day). No family holidays for her and no family pictures with my daughter being in them, and she loved her family so much.*
>
> *"Her family meant the world to her, especially after she became an aunt. Alina was in the delivery room welcoming her baby niece into this world. She said it was the most precious*

experience of her life. Now, a whole generation of my daughter is gone.

"My daughter was not sick and had no desire to leave this world this early.

"That individual, who is sitting right next to me, has decided to take everything away from my child whom I was carrying through life for twenty years.

"WHY?

"What did he want to accomplish by committing this evil act? He wanted to destroy her beauty. He wanted to remove her from this world.

"WHY?

"Alina was the most kind and loving, sweet girl. She loved living her life, and she loved the people around her. She loved every kind of person, no matter what race, color, religion. It seems she had a special connection with people because she was very compassionate and always wanted to help others. She participated in many fundraising events and loved service projects that benefited animals and children. Alina was brilliantly talented. She loved singing and dancing, and she was a great actress. She touched everyone's heart with her passion and beauty on stage. I had a special bond with my daughter. She was my best friend, my teacher, my inspiration.

"She was a pure, beautiful soul. And YOU, Darby, wanted to destroy that beauty. You wanted to destroy that young, beautiful woman who actually trusted you and cared so much for you!

"I want to quote what Alina said to me after HE broke into her house for the first time, and she was very upset by HIS actions and was so worried it could ruin HIS own life. 'Mom, I

don't know why he keeps making mistakes in his life, but he still is a good person, and he does not deserve to go to jail. I want to help him, Mom. I want to protect him.'

"But obviously things got worse, and she had to file a PFA. We were sitting in the courthouse, she was holding my hand, crying, and she said, 'Mom, I am very tired. I don't want any of that. I just want him to leave me alone. I had asked him so many times nicely, but he refused to understand. I still care for him, Mom, and I wish him the best in life. I just want him to leave me alone. He needs to understand that, Mom.'

"And he finally understood this and has decided to leave her alone. But in his own way. It seems he wanted to be very unique in his decision. No one could have predicted that uniqueness because no human being is able to be THAT unique.

"So, you, the evil right there, you really thought that destroying my daughter would make you feel happy and satisfied in life? Are you feeling happy now? Are you feeling satisfied by hurting so many people? So many hearts are broken. I believe the heart of your own mother is broken too. I'm sure your mother feels ashamed of her own son. She is probably ashamed to even be called a mother because she gave birth to a monster. I've learned that my daughter wanted to help you to become a better person in life. And she did believe in you.

"And all you wanted was to destroy her. But you failed! Darby, you failed!

"Her love for people has become even stronger. She is more alive than she has ever been; she is even more beautiful and powerful now. Alina is a beautiful angel. She brought so many people together by loving and supporting each other. She is guiding and helping us to make this world a better place. And as *long as the earth rotates on its axis, the world will be carrying her love and her beauty. And believe it or not, she still wants to help YOU.*

"She wants YOU to stay alive. She wants you to live a long life and think about what you have done because death is a part of a human, and she wants YOU to become a human first before your soul leaves this world.

"Our family is still grieving; we are still hurting. But grief, hurt, and pain are physical tools that our souls are using as stepping stones to enlightenment. Our family is getting stronger each day. We are trying our best to push through Alina's Law. Alina's Light is a nonprofit organization we have recently opened. We are planning to work with Alina's high school to create a scholarship fund and are going to organize different fundraising events to benefit children and animals to continue what our daughter loved doing.

"Alina's Light will be shining on earth forever."

Unlike my husband, from time to time, I would turn around and speak directly to Darby. Every time I did so, he was unblinkingly staring right into my eyes. I felt a very strong connection between him and my daughter. My daughter's soul communicated with him through my human body. And I felt that he heard her voice. He never said a word back though. But he had heard my daughter's last words to him. I felt his remorse, and I felt pity for him. I felt that my daughter was much better than him. I felt that my daughter's soul was vibrating at a much higher level than his. I felt that he was feeling that too. I felt that he was feeling how strong and powerful the soul of my daughter was compared to his, and I felt very sorry for his soul. I knew that the words of my daughter—the beautiful, young woman who was the only one who still cared for him and whom he had destroyed with his own hands—would be haunting him for the rest of his miserable life.

My son was the last person who presented a statement. He was very short with his words. He faced his sister's murderer for almost the whole length of his short speech. And a few times he got a warning to face the judge only. Artem said that Darby was a loser and a coward and that Darby got very lucky that they had never met. He said that if his sister had only said the word that she needed help, Darby would not be sitting there right now. In the end, he sarcastically wished Darby to have a great life in prison, and as he headed back to his seat, he turned around, pointed at Darby, and said, "See you soon."

The judge made a comment that it was the first time in his thirty years' experience that such a high-profile case had closed in such a short period of time. Then he pronounced his verdict, and Darby was escorted out of the courtroom. Neither Yan nor I looked at him as he left, but my mother-in-law watched carefully. She said that he could not take his eyes off us as if he were begging for forgiveness.

The night after the sentencing, Alina was in my dream. She looked beautiful and smiled. "Oh my God, Mom, good job at the courthouse. I am so proud of you. And I really like how you said to him, 'Goodbye, Matthew!' at the end. That was good."

I never said those last words to Darby. I just silently expressed with my eyes, "Goodbye, I'm glad you're not going to see my daughter any time soon," while I looked at him for the last time before I finished my statement and left.

I shared my dream with Becca the next day, and she could not believe it. She said that only Alina had called him "Matthew."

*   *   *

We were done with the process, and we were done with Darby. He was going to spend the rest of his life in prison, and we didn't want to occupy our minds with any thoughts pertaining to him. I was confused by life going on without Alina. I wanted closure, but there would never be any closure. Even though Darby was convicted and punished, my daughter was still dead. I felt as if I was starting a new chapter of life. The chapter of my life where there was no Alina anymore. My family had to continue our life book with all its pages about Alina ripped out. It felt very weird to make this book go on. Yan and I felt very lost.

We parented our daughter for twenty years, and it was impossible to suddenly stop doing it and move on. To have our sanity, we had to keep parenting Alina. Alina's Light, had become our child to parent now. We put all our energy and love into this organization. We wanted to honor our daughter by supporting those who share her passions, raise awareness, and promote education on domestic violence. Alina's Light is our survival.

Chapter 24: Past Life Regression

Grief is a process. To go through this process, you must let yourself feel every emotion that your mind and your body produce. After one year I had learned how to do it. Also, I had gotten to the point where I acknowledged what happened to my daughter and to our family. I was not rejecting, denying, or fighting it anymore. They say that the last stage of grief is acceptance. I didn't "accept" what had happened to my daughter. I would never accept that. I had just acknowledged that our lives would continue without Alina by our side. I had acknowledged that our lives would never be the same as before, and I had accepted that. I hated it with every fiber of my being. It hurt me. But I had accepted that pain and was not fighting anything anymore.

I acknowledged that I had faced the most difficult challenge that a human being could experience on earth. I knew that my soul needed that experience for some reason, and I wanted to know why.

Having been fascinated with Dr. Weiss's stories about the remarkable experiences of his patients during their past life regression sessions, I thought about having such a unique experience myself. I knew that past life regression was a popular and powerful tool for learning and healing. I really wanted to remember my previous life and see what relationship I had with Alina in it.

Meeting with Dr. Weiss required some travel, and there was a long waiting period. I had no patience, so I found a local therapist instead and was determined to give it a try. Dr. Turiano had over ten years' experience with past life regression and had good reviews. Without hesitation, I scheduled a session with him.

Yan brought me to his office and stayed in the car waiting for me. He had to wait for three hours.

I told the doctor about what was happening in my life and why I wanted his help. He was going to put me in a state of hypnosis and bring me to the life that had a direct connection with my current life issues. He told me that I would not be sleeping and that I would be fully aware of what was happening. He explained that I would be guided to access my memories through my subconscious mind, and he would direct me in my journey by asking questions. He said that I would need to simply describe what I saw and should not judge any scenes. I was very nervous and exited at the same time. I closed my eyes. The session started.

"OK, Elly, you're there. Look at your feet. What shoes are you wearing?"

I looked at my feet, and to my big surprise I saw that I was wearing dirty military boots.

"Are you male or female?"

I felt that I was a young man. I was 19 years old. I had blond hair. My name was Pavel. It felt very weird. At some point it felt as if I was making it up. I wondered why I would be seeing myself as a young man. I saw myself wearing a military coat and a hat with a Russian star on it. I tried not to think about what I was seeing and just follow the process.

"Where are you?"

I was at the field. It was very loud. I heard so much screaming. I was riding a horse, and I was holding a sword. I realized that I was a warrior, and a battle was taking place. I was a soldier in a cavalry army. I was a Bolshevik.

"Do you see any other people with you?"

I was surrounded by many other warriors. One was in front of us. He was screaming and encouraging us to go into battle. He was waving his sword wildly. I realized it was our commander.

"Do you recognize any of those people?"

I looked closer at our commander, and I could not believe the face I saw. That was my husband. Yan was my commander. I found it very funny, and I couldn't stop laughing. I was thinking, "What the heck... Yan is my commander... I am sick and tired of his commands in my current life."

Dr. Turiano asked what was happening and what I was seeing, but I could not see anything anymore. I got too distracted by laughing and judging Yan being there. I got embarrassed in front of my therapist and tried to be serious and cooperate.

"What do you see now? What's happening?"

I was riding a horse, screaming and waving my sword. Then I saw I had chopped off someone's head, and the head was rolling.

"What do you feel about it? Do you feel bad?"

I didn't feel bad at all. I said that I felt normal about it, and that's what I was at the battle for. I was there to fight and to kill. I kept riding my horse while watching that chopped head rolling.

What happened next, I could never have predicted. I came to therapy hoping to remember something nice and peaceful. I expected to remember something like I had been a queen, and my daughter had been a princess. If I were making things up, that's exactly what I would have probably fantasized. My next scene was something I never expected to see. I never would have made this up.

The chopped head stopped rolling and turned its face up. I saw the face of Alina. The person whom I had killed was my daughter in my current life. I screamed and cried, telling the therapist that I didn't understand why I was seeing Alina's face. I tried not to see that image. But the picture was very clear.

My therapist quickly directed me to change the scene so my panic would subside.

"Ok, go to the very last day of that life. What do you see?"

I immediately calmed down, and I saw myself as an old man with a gray beard. I was lying down on a beautiful field of grass. I felt very peaceful.

"Do you see yourself floating above your body?"

And I saw myself floating above that body of the old man.

"OK, you're there. You're in a spirit world. What do you see?"

I saw that Alina was there. We were holding hands and talking.

"What are you two talking about?"

Alina said that I had to go back and learn a lesson. She said she would help me. She said that I had to learn how to be more loving and compassionate. I was killing in my previous life, and I didn't care if that action was hurting other people. Now I needed to go back and experience that pain for myself. Alina said that she would be my daughter this time, but she would be taken from me too soon.

"Ok, now I'm going to ask you a very tough question. You can ignore it if you would like. Do you see the person who murdered your daughter in your current life?"

I immediately saw Darby there with us, and I said that yes, he was there.

"What do you feel?"

I didn't feel anything negative toward him. I was not mad or angry. I had a warm feeling inside me. I cried. I said, "I feel as if he were my son."

The session was over. I looked at my therapist with wide eyes and kept saying that I could not believe what I had just experienced. We talked about the spirit world for a while, and he gave me insights on what I had learned during my session. He expressed his deepest sympathy for my daughter and wished me the best in the journey of my current life.

I got into Yan's car and could not say a word. That was not what I had expected. I didn't even know how to tell him about who I had been in my past life. I was so embarrassed to tell him that I had killed my daughter and Darby had been my son.

Yan immediately realized that it didn't go well. I stayed silent for a few minutes, and he did not ask anything. My mind was spinning. But that was my past life, and I had to reveal it to Yan. I felt very emotional telling him about my experience. He did not say much to me; he didn't ask any questions and didn't judge. He just said, "Wow." Then he smiled and joked, "At least I was your commander... just don't kill me in this life please."

And since then, very often, when I get moody, he jokes with me, "Hey, Pavel, where is your horse?"

Chapter 25: Afterwards

After one year of grieving and learning about the spirit world, I was still dancing between two worlds. The spirit world had brought me peace. It felt as though I had found all the answers that my mind had been seeking. My mind had found a way out from that maze of the unresolvable issues of my life. The scary thoughts that my daughter was gone forever and that I would never see her again had shifted. I now fully grasped that my daughter being dead was only a temporary challenge I had to overcome. I realized that I was not going to face that challenge forever. One day it would all be over, and I would be with my daughter again. I knew it sounded insane to other people, but it had brought sanity to Yan and me.

"Never" and "forever" associated with my daughter did not sound as scary as it had before. It was still scary, but I knew it was not going to last forever. I realized that "never" and "forever" were only "temporary." That state of mind had tremendously reduced the severity of my panic attacks. Every time I panicked about my daughter being gone, I was able to shift to the feeling that my tough life here without my daughter was only a temporary thing, and realizing that she was waiting for me in the spirit world stopped my panic attack.

I had found where my daughter was and why she sacrificed herself in this life. I knew that my life was going to be tough until the last day. I knew that I had to learn the lesson of how to be more loving and compassionate.

I have become a completely different person. I see people with different eyes now. I feel people with my soul. I see a much bigger picture of people's lives today. I have become more loving and less judgmental. My daughter has profoundly changed me, and I am taking it as a valuable gift. She was always teaching me about life while she was here, and she is still teaching me about life now, even though she's gone. She is my teacher, my inspiration, my mentor. Now whenever I witness others around me enjoying their life and I get upset that my daughter is being deprived of that, I hear a voice in my head, saying, "It's OK, Mom, it has to be like that."

I truly believe that my soul needed to grow and evolve, and the soul of my daughter volunteered to help me. Also, I believe that the soul of my husband has volunteered to help me too by agreeing to be by my side. I would not have survived such a difficult life challenge without my husband being next to me. I truly believe that Yan is a very mature and experienced soul too. He is a caregiver and has a very loving nature. He has agreed to take on that challenge with me and help me go through it.

It took me almost a year to finish this book because I always felt emotional trying to put my feelings into words. I struggled so much with the English language, trying to explain and describe these scenes, but I always felt that my daughter was helping me put the right words down. With each chapter, I had to relive the reality of my daughter's death and all my experiences that came after. Writing about my feelings and experiences has been therapeutic and has helped me through my grieving process.

I wanted to share my experiences and help other grieving parents. I am still grieving. My husband is still grieving. Our family and friends are still grieving with us. We will be grieving the loss of our daughter until our last breath. But I wanted to give other parents the hope that our grief can be shifted to a different perspective. What seemed impossible for me to accept has become part of my life now, and I am able to find peace despite the devastation. What felt undoable has become my reality, and I am doing it every day. I wake up every morning and keep doing my undoable life without my child.

As I write this, we are approaching the second anniversary of Alina's transition. The second year has still been painful but different. While working on my book, I have been very busy with Alina's Light. We had the biggest celebration for our daughter's 22nd birthday. Alina's Light Walk for Love gathered about six hundred people at the park to remember her and celebrate her life. We awarded our first two scholarships to students from Alina's high school. Also, we have been supporting women's and animal shelters throughout the year and have made donations to a children's hospital. One of our goals is to support other women who are currently facing abusive situations. Alina's Light has been supporting and working toward getting Alina's Law passed to bolster the current protection-from-abuse laws.

Throughout the second year, we have worked hard, and our daughter has helped and guided us in every step of our new, uneasy life. Whenever the waves of grief hit hard and I feel discouraged and about to give up, I always read a letter from one of Alina's teachers that she sent me shortly after the day of the tragedy.

My name is Jamie Chiarelli. I was Alina's sixth grade math teacher at David E. Williams Middle School. Your daughter meant the world to me. I remember exactly where she sat. I remember her walking into my class being a shy, little, beautiful girl who never said much and had little confidence in her math skills. I remember her leaving my class as a beautiful, young girl with a smile on her face and as one of the best, if not the best, math students in the class.

I remember walking into the auditorium when Alina was in seventh grade and hearing her strong singing voice fill the room. I said to her, "Alina, did that big, powerful voice come out of that tiny body?" And with a smile from ear to ear, she nodded. What talent she did have. When she was on stage, her shyness faded into oblivion.

I know all too well that there is nothing I can write on this paper, there are no words I can offer to take away your pain. So I thought instead, I would offer you Alina's words. They were so precious to me, and I know anything of hers is precious to you.

I loved Alina. I love Alina. I will always love Alina.

Those words meant so much to me, and I always cried reading such heartfelt words about my little girl. Along with her letter Ms. Chiarelli had sent me Alina's essay that she had written as a sophomore. The title of the essay was "My Favorite Teacher." My child's words encouraged me to be strong and keep going with life.

Sixth grade was memorable only because of Mrs. Chiarelli. She is by far my favorite teacher that I have ever had so far. She made math fun! And that is very rare. She was hilarious and made the entire class laugh every day. Also, I can never forget her laugh. I remember how contagious it was. Her energy was the greatest though. She was always so lively and spirited that it made me excited to walk into her class.

Mrs. Chiarelli is one of the strongest women I know. In 2001, her barely 17-year-old son and his friend died in a car crash. They were star basketball players at Montour. Their deaths impacted everyone in the district. It surprises me how joyful she is after the tragic accident. Despite the devastation and heartbreak, she still manages to live the rest of her life with a positive attitude. She taught me to enjoy every day because you never know what can happen tomorrow.

I could read my daughter's words over and over again. They sounded like a personal message to me. Because she was amazed by the strength of her teacher who had lost her son, those words also encouraged me to be as strong as her teacher. I wanted my daughter to be proud of her mom. I wanted my daughter to be amazed by her mother's strength too. But the most important message I had noted in my daughter's words was that she wanted me to laugh and stay the cheerful mom I have always been.

Alina's two-year angel-versary was commemorated as A Musical Celebration of Love in her high school auditorium. As a tribute to our daughter, the school has placed a beautiful plaque in her memory on the wall by the auditorium. Alina's teachers and students from the various dance schools she had been a student of produced a beautiful concert in her memory.

Also, Yan and I have started attending monthly meetings with other bereaved parents in our area. In a few months, our lovely group will attend a second annual Helping Parents Heal conference that will take place in Charleston, SC. Hundreds of moms and dads will be getting together, sharing their stories about their beautiful children, and getting help from a healing crew. Many famous mediums, healers, therapists, and speakers are willing to dedicate their time, knowledge, talents, and passions to our unique club and help our healing process.

I don't get mad at other bereaved parents for smiling and laughing anymore. I smile and laugh with them now, and it does not mean that we have forgotten our children or don't love them. Laughing does not make me feel guilty now. I know that every time I laugh, my daughter is laughing with me.

In a few months, I am going to take a two-day mediumship course with my favorite medium, Suzanne Giesemann, who is coming to Pittsburgh.

The connection with my daughter is becoming stronger each day, and I'm very proud to reveal that I got another tattoo. Two hearts on my left arm: "Mother and Daughter Forever."

*   *   *

People might think that I am strong because I don't want the death of my child to define me. But that would be a false statement. I am strong because the death of my daughter defines every single aspect of my life. I am who I am because my daughter has lived and because my daughter has died.

The spirit of my daughter is shining so brightly. I know her light will never dim. I loved my daughter when she lived, and my love has become even stronger after she died. Love never dies. The power of love can do miracles. It connects two worlds. The power of love connects us with our loved ones in the spirit world. That world is beautiful, and I look forward to finishing all my uneasy lessons here as an "A" student by making this world a better place and joining my daughter as a high-vibrating soul.

If I were asked to give advice to a newly bereaved mother or father, I would say that there is no advice. I would only say that it's OK to be emotional. I would ask you to acknowledge your feelings and validate your thoughts and emotions. The hardest part would then be to let those feelings go. Do not feel like you need to keep the sadness. Remember that the strongest energy and connections to all realms and dimensions come from love.

Self-care is very important, so try to override the negative thoughts with a prayer or meditation or even a hobby. It's vital to occupy your brain with something, anything, that brings you even the slightest joy—walking, cooking, reading, watching a movie, just something that triggers the release of natural endorphins, which in turn helps heal the emotional pain and trauma. Unfortunately, there is no time frame or ultimate understanding of grief. All you can do is just trust the process and live.

From my own experience, if you're a newly bereaved mother or father, I know nothing would sound right to you and no advice would be needed. But please believe that your soul and your body know what to do. Just be open and listen to your soul. Your beautiful soul will lead you, and you will find your way, your own unique way.

With the guidance of my daughter, I have found mine.

Alina's Story

Alina was born in Ivanovo, Russia, and her family moved to the United States when she was 3 years old. Alina was brilliantly talented; she loved singing, dancing, and acting. She touched the hearts of many with her passion and beauty on stage.

Alina developed her passion for the performing arts at a very early age. Her journey started at the European School of Rhythmic Gymnastics when she was 4 years old. At the age of 5, she was performing solo numbers in out-of-state competitions. In elementary school, she was a student of Tammy Lee's School of Dance, where she obtained starring roles, performing acrobatic dance numbers. In a short period of time, Alina learned dance styles and skills that would take years for most children to master. Because of her exceptional talent, she was privileged to perform in a group of much older, more experienced dancers.

In 5th grade, Alina joined the Karen Prunzik Broadway Dance Studio. She became adept at multiple styles of dance, including hip-hop, tap, and ballet. True to her Russian heritage, she even served as prima ballerina for the studio. She competed at On Stage New York and Access Broadway and won multiple awards for her outstanding performances. Throughout the years, Alina also performed at several local Pittsburgh events including Light Up Night, Macy's Christmas parades, and various events in Robinson Township, Kennywood, and Idlewild Park. Additionally, the confidence that she developed through dance allowed Alina to discover her talent as a singer. She brought audiences to tears with her beautiful renditions of many well-known songs, both on stage in front of an audience and at home with her family.

When Alina was 14 years old, she suffered a severe knee injury during a ballet class and underwent major surgery. After months of physical therapy, Alina received the heartbreaking news that she would not be able to dance competitively or recreationally again. Despite this major setback, she was committed to returning to the stage and was determined to find a way. While at Montour High School, Alina was a member of the musical theater group through which she was able to safely exhibit her passion for dance. Alina returned to the stage as a gifted actress, dancer, vocalist, and comedian, shining her light and love on the audience. She starred in several musicals and plays, bringing tears, smiles, and much applause. Alina was also part of the chorus at Montour, and she performed at many events across the city and continued to shine her light and bring joy to all in attendance.

Although Alina's injury prevented her from pursuing her passion as a dancer and performer, her treatment experience inspired her to pursue a career in the medical field. She wanted to help others who had suffered injuries that prevented them from pursuing their dreams. Alina decided that she wanted to become a doctor of physical therapy.

Alina graduated from Montour High School in 2015 and spent the first two years of her college career at the University of Pittsburgh-Greensburg. She lived in the Outdoor Adventure & Community Service (OACS) living community during her time at Pitt-Greensburg.

In fact, she was the vice president of OACS during the spring semester of 2017. She loved participating in an organization that benefited animals and children. Again, Alina continued to shine her light, touching the lives of people and animals with her love and attention.

Alina then transferred to the University of Pittsburgh's Oakland campus. She lived with her friends in an apartment and was prepared to dedicate herself to becoming a doctor of physical therapy.

However, on October 8, 2017, Alina was senselessly and tragically killed at the young age of 20. One year later, in October 2018, Alina's murderer was sentenced to life in prison. But Alina's light was not extinguished. Her legacy of love, kindness, and compassion will continue to shine, and the world will always be brighter because Alina was part of it.

Alina deeply treasured her family, including her father, Yan; her mother, Elly; her brother, Artem; her sister-in-law, Kate; and her niece, Angelina. Alina was so excited for the birth of her niece, and she was even present in the delivery room when Angelina was born. In the short amount of time they were able to spend together, Alina and Angelina formed a special bond. Alina also had a special bond with her mother, who she referred to as her best friend. Alina loved and valued her entire family immensely, including her family in Russia. She visited her family in Russia and became even prouder of her Russian heritage. Although her family misses her desperately, the Sheykhets are proud of the legacy that Alina has left and the light she has brought into this world.

Alina was an exceptional young woman. She radiated love, life, and energy. She had a compassionate spirit that made everyone around her feel special. She had a remarkable smile that brightened every room she entered. She had a contagious laugh that made everyone feel like they were in on the joke. She was not just alive; she was living. This world and the people in it were blessed to have the opportunity to bask in her vibrancy. Alina was a beautiful person, and her spirit is still here on earth guiding and inspiring us.

Alina's Light was created to honor Alina's life and light by supporting the causes that were important to her as well as raising awareness and promoting education on topics relating to domestic violence. Alina's Light will also promote the passage and implementation of laws and policies that protect victims of domestic violence, such as Pennsylvania House Bill 588, which has been titled "Alina's Law."

To learn more about Alina and her story, please visit www.alinaslight.com

Your support and donations are greatly appreciated.

A Note from Becca Kubiczki

According to the Partnership Against Domestic Violence, every nine seconds, a woman in the U.S. is assaulted or beaten. Every nine seconds, a woman is at risk at the hands of someone who is supposed to love and protect her. But domestic violence is one of those topics that we as a society choose to ignore. If we ignore it, it can't happen to us. If we pretend it isn't happening to others, it could never happen to our loved ones.

Until it does. On October 8th, 2017, I learned the harsh reality that domestic violence does not discriminate. It is an epidemic that does not care how beautiful you are, how intelligent you are, or how well you were raised. Alina, my college roommate and close friend, lost her life. Suddenly, one of my loved ones joined the harsh statistics.

The day I met Alina, I knew I found a forever friend. It was the first day of my first year of college. She quickly became my right hand, my confidant, the one I could go to for anything. The one I could laugh about nothing with for hours at a time on my dorm floor (usually fueled by a bottle of New Amsterdam).

After she died, milestones suddenly became bittersweet. Five months after I lost Alina, I celebrated my 21st birthday. Eighteen months after I lost Alina, I graduated college. Losing a friend at a young age, especially in such a horrific way, changes the way you view life. It forced me to wonder what I could have said and done differently and where I "went wrong." I blamed myself for what happened. I blamed myself for certain loved ones being there that morning and what they went through. I will always wish that I could take that pain away from them. I wondered if things would have turned out differently if I had been a little bit more assertive or a little bit more patient. I felt immense guilt for the way that she lost her life and believe that a little bit of that guilt will always linger.

Unfortunately, I cannot change what happened. All I can do is move forward and make positive changes in her name. This isn't something to just "get over"; it is something that I will have to face every day, some more than others. Instead of dwelling, I choose to be happy, because, as cliché as it sounds, I know that is what she wants. Throughout the court process and every day after that, I have been reminded that Alina is so much more than a victim and a statistic. She was an amazing person with a meaningful life—one worth fighting for, one that can make a difference. Not a day goes by where I don't think of my friend, but when I see little signs like a butterfly, a cardinal, or the color purple, I know she is thinking of me too.

A Note from Sasha Phillips

I only really met Alina a few days before she was gone. I was an attorney assigned to the Protection From Abuse case against her ex-boyfriend. My first impression told me that this is a very bright, eloquent, and beautiful young woman, and as we talked, this impression was confirmed. I remember thinking that very few people are like her — beautiful inside and out. Her mom was there with her — just as beautiful and sweet.

I really don't want to think about the following Monday when I got the news. That's beyond my worst nightmare. To say I was devastated is to say nothing. Seeing Alina's mom at a funeral was probably the hardest thing I'd ever done, considering my oldest daughter is just a few years younger than Alina. I just couldn't come to terms with this horrible incident and with all the "what ifs" that kept popping up in my mind. I kept thinking, "What can I do? There has to be something." I got my answer almost instantly from Alina, I think.

At Alina's funeral, a girl came up and handed me Alina's picture. I had no idea who that girl was; she never introduced herself. Then a canvas I forgot on the top shelf of my studio fell literally into my hands. Then a tube of red paint I ordered months ago and forgot about suddenly came. Then, when I wasn't sure what to do with the hands, I dreamed a girl was standing and holding fire in her hands. When I thought I couldn't paint it because I didn't have a photo to work from, a photo of flame popped up on my phone—I have no idea where it came from. Everything was pushing me first toward painting and then towards creating a very particular image — it was as if I was just a conduit for someone else's message. A window in the background turned out looking like a halo, (and I just happened to find a book of gold leaf I misplaced a while ago); Alina's gaze in the picture changed after a light bulb exploded above the portrait (!) and I had to fix the smudges left by the glass on the eyes; and deep red shadows appeared on her face after a brush loaded with red paint accidentally fell out of my hands and marked up the painting. The portrait kept coming together through my dreams and through "coincidences," and then I pushed to finish it after an invitation to participate in the Kassia Ensemble "Women's Voices" exhibit (which confirmed to me that Alina really wanted her voice to be heard).

And here is the rest of the story. At that art exhibit, I met another attorney with whom we ultimately decided to form a group that promotes art as a form of wellness and therapy for professionals without any art training. This is also not a coincidence. As I think of Alina and her story of injury, which ultimately made her decide to become a physical therapist, I'm now even more convinced that her spirit is very much here, determined to help people in every way she can. Before I met her, I really had no idea art therapy existed. Painting this portrait gave me so much peace and healing, but what's more, it connected me with several people who are now promoting art and music therapy as a way for people to cope with stress and traumatic events.

And so this story continues — on the second anniversary of Alina's death, her portrait received an invitation to participate in the Biennale Venezia's Art Against Violence, and I was given the honor of telling her story at the art show and at the attorney round table scheduled for the day of the exhibit's inauguration.

Poems by Elly Sheykhet

I COULDN'T HAVE SURVIVED WITHOUT YOU

When I wake in the morning, I ask myself
How will I get through this day WITHOUT YOU?
Then you push me out of bed and whisper
That I need to make another step FOR YOU.

As I dress and prepare to start my day, I wonder
How will I go on WITHOUT YOU?
Then I remember your smile and hear your voice
That I need to make another day FOR YOU.

I step outside and I ask myself
How can I enjoy the sun WITHOUT YOU?
Then I feel your arms around me, and I hear
"Don't worry, Mom, I will help YOU."

I smile with tears in my eyes, and I look up
Then I see the cloud shaped as a perfect HEART.
I see you dancing in the sky and singing,

"Mom, we're still together, we aren't APART."

As I drive my car, I cry, and I think
There is no road that can lead my car to YOU.
Then I see a 77 vehicle in front of me
"I am here, Mom. I am still with YOU."

I turn the radio on, and I hear,
"Hey, beautiful, beautiful, beautiful, beautiful Angel
Love your imperfections every angle
Tomorrow comes and goes before you know
So, I just had to let you know."

I come to my office, and I stare at every picture of YOU.
I turn on my computer, and I sigh
ALINA, I can't work without thinking of YOU
My computer starts flicking, and I hear your laugh,
"Go finish your project, Mom, don't make it that rough."

I go for a walk at lunch, and I wonder
How can I walk on that beautiful trail WITHOUT YOU?
Then I hear a sound of a bike, and the voice warns,
"Excuse me, I am here, right BEHIND YOU."

Then I see a squirrel running toward ME,

I reach out my hand to it, and it's not afraid of ME.

It sits still and stares with its beautiful eyes at ME

I'm mesmerized, I can hear, "Hi, Mom, it's ME!"

I pick up my granddaughter, and I wonder

How can I enjoy your niece WITHOUT YOU?

Then Angelina smiles, she looks at me, and I hear,

"Mom, through Angelina's eyes, I can still look at YOU."

I watch Angelina playing in the car, and I ask myself

How can I ever be happy here WITHOUT YOU?

Then Angelina points her little finger at the empty seat and laughs

"I'm the one who makes her laugh, Mom, I'm here WITH YOU."

At the end of the day as I prepare to close my eyes

I know I could not have gotten through the day WITHOUT YOU.

Then I close my eyes, and I hear your voice

"You survived another day, Mom, good night, I am so proud of
        YOU."

DOMESTIC VIOLENCE IS REAL

Love shouldn't hurt and shouldn't kill
Domestic violence is real.
As real as those pictures are
Alina is not where you are.

She loved, she laughed, she lived
The mental abuse wasn't perceived.
It was a silly love mind game
But she was burning from its flame.

Was not aware of such a deal
Domestic violence was so real.
Was not aware life wasn't sealed
Was not aware she could be killed.

Please be aware of that flame
Abuse is real; it's not a game.
Please recognize the abuser's sign
I am the best; you're only mine.

You can be short; you can be tall
You can be pretty as a doll.

Elly Sheykhet

Abuse cannot define you
You hide, but it might find you.

It doesn't care if you're black or white
It doesn't care if you have a right.
Alina's Light will tell you that
Please be aware and wear her hat.

Please be aware of her light
Alina's Light is shining bright.
Love shouldn't hurt and shouldn't kill
Domestic violence is real.

If you're a victim of abuse's flame
Please ask for help with no shame.
There is no chance for silent break up
Please be aware you need to speak up.

Love shouldn't hurt and shouldn't kill
Alina's Light is for you to heal.

I WILL GRIEVE FOR THE REST OF MY LIFE

I will grieve for the rest of my life.
 But I know my daughter helps me survive.
 She is holding my hand and helping to go.
 Go forward in life that is now windblown.

She was never afraid to deal with difficult times.
 She was always brave to face the ugly rhymes.
 She is still very brave and very strong.
 She shows how to continue to do no wrong.

She's channeled my pain into a different course.
 My story has become someone's survival source.
 My life is helping others to overcome their fears.
 My life is helping others to deal with their tears.

The meaning of my grieving is very deep.
 The life path I continue to walk is so steep.
 But I am not afraid of feeling any scars.
 My daughter is leading me through thorns to the stars...

Elly Sheykhet

MY GREATEST LOVE, MY GREATEST PAIN

You're my greatest love, my greatest pain.
Your sudden death was not in vain.
I am forever changed forever broken
My heart is cracked and widely open

It's open for change, its open for love
To breathe my new life in is very tough
Each breath in hurts but teaches life
It teaches how to love and survive.

It's open for learning, for new understanding
My soul is screaming, my soul is demanding
Demanding to know my purpose of living
I am feeling enlightened and I am believing.

THE SHOW MUST GO ON

The stage, the light, the applause
She wears a beautiful blouse
Last song, last dance, last bow
She cries, it was her last show...

My grief is the art of living
Living with a wound and believing
Believing that her show must go on
Bleeding but keeping her lights always on

Grief is a painful and beautiful art
I sing and dance with my bleeding heart
Even she has left, even she has gone
I know her show must go on

Elly Sheykhet

About the Author

Elly Sheykhet grew up in Ivanovo, Russia. In 2000, she moved with her husband Yan and two children, Artem and Alina, from Russia to Pittsburgh, Pa.

After losing her daughter in 2017, Elly developed a different understanding of life and death and hopes that her book will help others who suffer the loss of a loved one.

Elly is very passionate about Alina's Light, a charitable organization formed in memory of her daughter. She dedicates her life to honor her daughter by helping others who share Alina's passions.

To learn more about Alina's Light, please visit www.alinaslight.com. Elly can be reached at sheykhet@alinaslight.com.

Made in the USA
Middletown, DE
10 August 2020

15009274R00128